W9-AJL-539

The Sound *of* Silence

The Sound *of* Silence

Growing Up Hearing with Deaf Parents

Myron Uhlberg

Albert Whitman & Company
Chicago, Illinois

Library of Congress Cataloging-in-Publication data is on file with the publisher.

Text copyright © 2019 by Myron Uhlberg
Hardcover edition first published in the United States of America
in 2019 by Albert Whitman & Company
ISBN 978-0-8075-3146-4

This work is based on *Hands of My Father: A Hearing Boy, His Deaf Parents,
and the Language of Love*, originally published by Bantam Books, a division of
Random House, a subsidiary of Penguin Random House, in 2009.

Printed in the United States of America
10 9 8 7 6 5 4 3 2 1 LB 24 23 22 21 20 19

Cover art copyright © 2019 by Albert Whitman & Company
Cover art by Carolyn Arcabascio
Interior design by Aphee Messer

For more information about Albert Whitman & Company,
visit our website at www.albertwhitman.com.

100 years of Albert Whitman & Company
Celebrate with us in 2019!

In memory of my parents, Louis and Sarah Uhlberg

Their grandchildren, Eric, Robin, and Ken

Their great-grandchildren,
Alexandra, Kelli, Max, and Miles

With deepest gratitude to my wife, Karen

And in memory of my brother, Irwin

PART I

Apt. 3A

CHAPTER 1

Dramatic Welcome

I've never liked being the center of attention. But in my family, I always have been, ever since I was born just after midnight on July 1, 1933.

Everything about that day was peculiar. For one, I came into this world during one of the biggest electrical thunderstorms in the history of Brooklyn, New York, where my parents lived. According to my father, on the night of my birth, giant fingers of lightning reached down from the sky and ignited oil tanks, which exploded, sending flames hundreds of feet into the sky and turning night into day. Then the clouds cracked open, releasing a flood of water on our neighborhood and turning Brooklyn's wide avenues into raging rivers.

In the middle of all this chaos, my father ran out of Coney Island Hospital, where my mother was about to give birth, and howled at the sky like a banshee.

People sometimes say I get dramatic. I think it might be because of the dramatic circumstances of my birth. But there was another reason I was the center of attention that night. You see, both of my parents were deaf, and no one, not even the doctors, could say if I would be born deaf too.

When I finally arrived, the first words my father spoke to me, as I lay in my mother's arms, were with his hands. As a deaf man, my father had no words to speak. Instead, he introduced me into the world with joyous signs of welcome. His hands flashed in the air, quivering with excitement: "Welcome! Welcome! Open your eyes! You are home now." And in the same way that many children start learning to speak from the moment their mother whispers "I love you" into their little ears, I began to learn my first language by watching my father's hands through half-closed eyes.

My father was right. I was home. But unlike my parents, I could also hear the murmuring voices and the thunder outside the hospital window. And while I stepped with one foot into my parents' silent world, my other tiny foot was born into another world. The world that I would one day call my own.

CHAPTER 2

A New Addition

My parents' world was a four-room apartment on the third floor of a redbrick building, not far from Coney Island. And on certain summer days, when the wind was blowing just right and our kitchen window was open, I could smell the salty air of the Atlantic Ocean, sometimes even catching a hint of mustard and grilled hot dogs from Nathan's Famous hot dog stand (although this part may have been my imagination).

On one of these afternoons, when I was old enough to understand sign, my father told me about the events that led him to plead to the sky on that crazy night. It was his story. But it is also the beginning of my story.

As always, my father spoke with his hands. His hands were his voice. And his hands contained his memories.

Like me, my father was born hearing. But at an early age, he had become very ill, so ill that his parents thought he would die. Fever ravaged his body for more than a week. And when it finally let up, he was alive, but he would never hear another sound for the rest of his life.

"Not fair!" he signed to me, his hands fast, angry. I could always tell, at a glance, my father's moods—happy, angry, thoughtful, playful, serious—by paying careful attention to the way he signed. The signs sent the information, but the way he signed them told me more, like how an actor could make a character come alive, not by the words he said but by the way he said them.

My father told me that because both of his parents could hear, he could barely communicate with them. He shared only a few signs with his father: *eat, be quiet, sleep*. Each one was a command sign. There was no sign for *love* between them.

My father did share a sign for *love* with his mother.

It was a home-sign, a sign she had created, and she used it often. My father told me that his language with his mother was poor in quantity but rich in content. She communicated less through signs than through the glow that appeared in her eyes whenever she looked at him. That look was special, for him alone.

When he was eight years old, my father was sent to live at the Fanwood School for the Deaf, a military-style school for deaf children. He thought his parents had abandoned him—that he was damaged. In his early days, he cried himself to sleep every night. But slowly he realized that he had not been abandoned. He had been rescued. For the first time in his life, he was surrounded by children just like him. He finally saw that he was not alone.

But the education he received at Fanwood was a mixed blessing. There, as at most deaf schools at the time, the children were taught by hearing teachers. So instead of teaching the students sign, the teachers tried to teach them speech.

Being deaf does not mean that a person is mute. The deaf have vocal cords and can speak. But they cannot hear the sounds of their voices, so teaching them spoken English is very difficult. Although my father and his classmates tried to cooperate with their teachers, not one of them ever learned to speak well enough to be understood by the average hearing person.

To make things worse, sign language was forbidden. The hearing teachers thought sign was a primitive way of communicating, only for the unintelligent. It was not until many years later that American Sign Language (ASL) was recognized as the legitimate, expressive language that it is. But long before then, my father and his friends came to that conclusion themselves. Every night, in the dormitory at Fanwood, the older deaf children taught the younger ones the visual language of sign.

"When I was a boy, I had no real signs," my father told me, his hands moving, remembering. "I only had made-up home-signs. These were like shadows on a wall. They had no real meaning. In deaf school I was hungry for sign. All were new for me. Sign was the food that fed me. Food for the eye. Food for the mind. I swallowed each new sign to make it mine."

My father learned the printing trade in school. He

was told this was a perfect trade for the deaf because printing can be a very noisy business. But the message he received from the hearing teachers was that the deaf were not as smart, or capable, as hearing students, so they had to be taught skills, such as printing, shoe repair, and house painting.

When he graduated, my father got his first and only job.

"I was lucky to have an apprentice job with the *New York Daily News*," he told me. "I knew it was because I was deaf, and so wouldn't be distracted by the noise of the printing presses, but I didn't care. I also didn't care that the deaf workers were paid less than the hearing workers, because Captain Patterson, the big boss, knew that we wouldn't, couldn't, complain. He knew that we would be happy for any job, at any wage. We were deaf. He could hear. And he was right."

Here my father paused, and his hands lay still on his lap while he remembered. "The hearing people ran the world," he signed, his hands moving in sadness.

After many years as an apprentice, my father earned his union card. This meant that his job was protected, and for him, it was proof that he was as good as any hearing man.

In the darkest days of the Great Depression, almost one of every four men in the United States did not have a job. The numbers were even worse for the deaf, since not many were employed in skilled trades. Luckily for my father, people kept buying newspapers during the Depression, probably hoping to read of good news that the hard times were ending. Because of this, my father kept his job, and he earned enough money to support a family.

"I wanted a partner forever," my father told me. His finger formed a circle like a clock, then his hand moved forward, showing the endless passage of time that was *forever*.

Before long, my father met my mother, Sarah. She had been born hearing too, but like so many kids in the early 1900s, before antibiotics had been discovered, she came down with scarlet fever. And when she recovered, she had lost her hearing. She had just turned one year old. Just as was the case with my father's hearing family, not one of her parents or her siblings had learned any real signs. They had barely communicated with her, using simple homemade gestures.

"We would be two deaf people in the hearing world," my father told me. "We would make our own world. A quiet world. A silent world."

After getting married, my father and mother found our apartment near Coney Island. They negotiated the price with the hearing landlord by themselves, even though their parents said that they "could not manage alone" because they were "deaf and handicapped" and would surely "be cheated."

Nine months later, at the bottom of the Great Depression, I was born. My parents had overcome many things together, but they now faced one of their greatest challenges yet: raising a hearing son.

"When Mother Sarah was struggling to bring you into this world," my father signed, his fingers fluttering, his hands spewing out a flood of words. "And the sky was split in half, like a black egg, cracked apart with blinding streaks of light, I rushed out into an underwater world, out into the downpour, screaming my questions into the heavens." Then he paused. Thinking. And he smiled. His hands came to life. "We would manage," he signed. "Together. We would build a life together."

CHAPTER 3

The Tests

My parents had little help in trying to figure out how to raise me. Because there was no common way for the hearing and deaf to communicate other than writing notes, the two worlds were almost completely cut off from each other. My parents worried this meant that they would be cut off from me.

"How would we know when you cried in the dark?" my father's hands asked. "When you were hungry? Happy? Sad? When you had a pain in your stomach?"

"And how," he signed, "would we tell you we loved

you?" My father's hands became still, thoughtful.

"I was afraid I would not know you if you were a hearing baby. I feared you would not know your deaf father." Then he smiled. "Mother Sarah was not worried. She said she was your mother. She would know you. There was no need for mouth speak. No need for hand speak."

The first order of business was to make sure everything was normal with my hearing. This might sound strange, but neither of my parents' families were quite sure how they had gone deaf. They knew my mother and father had been sick, but to my grandparents, the illness and the deafness were not necessarily connected. After all, their other children had gotten sick from time to time, and they had not gone deaf. They did not have "broken ears."

My father continued. "When we brought you home from the hospital, we arranged for Mother Sarah's family to come to our apartment every Saturday afternoon. 'Urgent!' I wrote. 'You must come! Every week. Saturday.'

"They listened. They came from Coney Island every weekend for your first year of life. They never missed, all of them: Mother Sarah's mother and father, and her younger sister and three younger brothers. They ate like horses, but it was worth it."

"How boring that must have been for them," I signed, pressing my finger to my nose, mimicking the monotonous turning of a grindstone wheel.

"We didn't care," he signed vigorously. "I had a plan!

"They always came when you were sleeping. I made sure of that. Before making themselves comfortable, I asked them to stand at the back of your crib. Then they pounded on pots and pans I gave them. You heard a big noise and snapped awake, and you began to wail. It was a wonderful sight to see you cry so strongly at the heavy sound."

"Wonderful?" I asked. "Wonderful for who?" No wonder I had trouble sleeping some nights, I thought.

My father continued, ignoring my complaint.

"On Sundays, my mother, father, brother, and two sisters came down from the Bronx. They did not trust Mother Sarah's family. They brought their own pots and pans." Here, my father's hands formed a small curved pot, then they traced a larger pot that could hold a dozen potatoes. Then, seamlessly, his hand grasped an imaginary handle of an enormous frying pan, moving it back and forth over an equally imaginary, but very hot, flame.

"Each one held a pot or a pan on their lap during the two-hour, three-subway-ride trip from way up in the Bronx, to Kings Highway in Brooklyn. They practiced banging on the pots and pans while the subway cars went careening through the tunnels. The train's wheels made such a screeching sound that people on the car barely noticed them. When they got off the subway, my sisters and brother marched to our apartment, still banging the pots and pans. They looked like some ragtag army in a Revolutionary War painting." My father's signs were so expressive, so lifelike, that I could see each one in my mind's eye. First was my heavyset uncle, plodding up the street with a determined look on his face, banging away on a pot big enough to cook a large chicken. Then, trailing behind were my stern aunts, smacking their frying pans with soup ladles.

"As soon as they arrived at our apartment," my father continued, "they hid behind the head of your bed and pounded away while they stomped their feet like a marching band. I felt the noise through the soles of my feet. They had a nice rhythm. The result was the same: you awoke immediately. Jumped, actually."

"How about our neighbors?" I asked. "All that banging and stomping. Didn't they mind?"

"What do you expect?" my father answered. "We had to know if your hearing stayed with you. The neighbors threatened to call the landlord. Have us evicted. Mother Sarah sweet-talked them out of it. The notes flew fast and furious between her and the neighbors till they settled down. Anyway, they thought you were a cute baby. They were not completely convinced that you could hear. They wondered if the deaf can have a hearing baby. We were the only deaf people they knew. They had no idea of our deaf ways."

I watched as his hands added, striking each other sharply, "It was hard for Mother Sarah and me to figure out how to take care of you. But we did. We learned how to tell when you cried at night. You slept in your crib next to our bed when we brought you home from the hospital. We kept a small light on all night. Mother Sarah wore a ribbon attached to her wrist and to your little foot. When you moved, she would immediately awake to see the reason why. She still has that ribbon somewhere. Sign was your first language. The first sign you learned was *I love you*.

"That is a good sign. The best sign."

CHAPTER 4

A Fox in Brooklyn

As I grew, the ribbon around my arm disappeared, and I slowly began to learn to tell my parents what I needed through sign. And along with my signing ability, my own memories began to form. One of the first signs I can remember learning was for the question *What?*

This is an essential word in sign. It's so important there are actually two signs for it. Both are dramatic, and they are often used together for added forcefulness. Nearly every exchange between my parents and me in my early years began with them asking me this question.

My answer would tell them many things: My needs. My feelings. My emotions. My state of mind. The sign left no room for doubt. The right finger would pass over each finger of the left hand, from index to pinkie, listing, while asking, "Which one?"

With this information, my parents would be able to figure out what to do next. But it always started with my response to that question, which concluded with the second, more insistent sign: *What? WHAT?* This time both hands were thrown out, palms up, moving back and forth. They demanded, *Come on, what do you want?* Meanwhile, the face formed a puzzled look like a crinkled walnut, and the shoulders rose in anticipation, along with the eyebrows, wrinkling the forehead.

My earliest memory of this sign takes place when I was still too young to have a room of my own. I awoke to a sound coming from my parents' closet. Frightened, I got out of my crib and walked in my footed pajamas to wake my father.

He jerked upright as I shook his shoulder. "What?" he asked, his hands wiggling back and forth, demanding an answer. His face was twisted with puzzlement, and his shoulders were hunched up, waiting.

"WHAT?" His follow-up sign demanded that I respond. Since he was deaf and I could hear, he could not allow any misunderstanding between us. The answer had to be exact, the danger clear, the need for action immediate.

But on this night, at midnight, the *what* was my fear—what was the sound that woke me up?

I pointed to my ear and banged my fists together, the sign for *I heard a noise*. To make sure my father knew that it was a scary noise, I beat my fists hard against each other. My father stilled my hands and got out of bed.

"Show me," he signed.

For a moment, I didn't know how to respond. How could I *show* him a sound? I decided to show him where the noise was coming from. Taking his hand, I pointed to the closet.

As I stood clinging to his leg, my father opened the closet door. There, staring down at me, I saw my nightmare come to life. Perched on shelf in the closet, I saw the hairy, evil face of a fox. Its bright, hungry, unblinking eyes stared straight into mine.

I was frozen, terrified. I saw the fox hunching its shoulders, preparing to spring down onto me. Its lips curled back revealing a mouthful of white, pointy teeth.

I screamed for my mother, but she slept on, her back turned to the sight of her only child about to be eaten alive. *Doesn't she care?* I wondered. My mind could not understand the fact that she could not hear the fox's hungry snarl or my terrified cries.

Seeing my panic, my father grabbed the fox and yanked it from its perch. Shaking the thing back and forth, he squeezed it tight, and soon the creature's eyes turned glassy. The fox hung limp, tail down, in my father's strong hands. Then, for good measure, my father slammed it down on the closet floor.

"Don't be afraid," his hands said, fluttering wildly over his heart with the sign for *fear*. "This fox won't bother you anymore." I was still scared stiff, until my father knelt down to me and looked straight into my eyes, while his hands turned over and lay still. "This fox is dead!" his hands assured me. Then, leaving no doubt in my frightened mind, his hands curled up into two V's, like the fox's legs sticking up in the air. They wriggled once and curled up into his palms, silenced. And sure enough, the fox lay at my feet, lifeless.

Wiping the tears from my eyes, my father led me back to my bed. As he tucked me tightly under my quilt, he looked at me for the longest time, a half smile on his lips. Then he gave me a soft kiss goodnight, and I went back to sleep.

For many years, I tried to make sense of what happened that night. Surely, there was no wild fox running around in Brooklyn. At least, not on my block. Not in apartment 3A. And certainly, not in my parents' closet.

It wasn't until I was older that I realized the terrible creature of my nightmares had never been alive at all. The monster my father had killed for me that night had been my mother's fox-fur wrap—the garment she wore with her fanciest dresses.

My father did not have the language to tell me what was going on that night. But I knew that the look on his face as he tucked me back in was special, for me alone. And that said more than any sign could.

CHAPTER 5

Learning to Listen

My second language was spoken English.

I don't remember learning to speak, but somehow, some way, I did. Because my parents were deaf, they did not try to teach me spoken language, but that did not mean that our home was quiet. In addition to the weekly banging of pots and pans through the first year of my life, there was a radio, which filled my room with music, and the music of speech.

My father was convinced, since there was no one to tell him otherwise, that a person gained and maintained the ability to hear through practice—like a weight lifter keeps their muscles strong by exercising. So he decided shortly after bringing me home from the hospital that hearing was something I would learn. And once I learned it, he would not allow me to lose it through disuse.

The radio he bought to ensure my constant exposure to sound sat on a small stand by the head of my bed, just beyond the wooden slats of my crib. It was turned on day and night. And the warm yellow light and the soft sound pouring from that wood and cloth box comforted me as I fell asleep.

When I left my crib for a bed with no sides, alongside my new grown-up bed in my very own room was a new grown-up radio. I had graduated from a table model to a solid piece of dark wooden furniture that sat heavily on my bedroom floor. It was taller than me and looked like a cathedral, with an arched dome and a decorative face that was filled with cloth instead of stained glass.

There wasn't any *eureka* moment in my learning to speak English, but I am sure that the radio playing constantly alongside my head helped my brain crack the code of speech in my otherwise speechless world.

As I listened, I would catch my father studying me, questioning whether I could still hear. Whenever he did this, I'd peek under the rag rug in our living room, pretending to be looking for my lost hearing. He didn't think this was as funny as I did, and his response was always our home-sign for *wise guy*.

Our radio became like a Rosetta stone to my father. He seemed to hope that by looking closely enough at this sound-making object, he would be able to better understand the sound he could not hear. But unlike the Rosetta stone, my radio had no symbols that could be turned into language. It just had a light, a dial with some numbers, and an arrow that settled from time to time on those numbers—some more often than others.

My father struggled to understand how the radio worked, because to him it just sat there on the floor doing nothing. So he removed the back and studied the many tubes inside. He noted how they flickered on like candles, wavered, and then burned brightly, steadily.

"Beautiful, but it's not meant for us deaf," he signed matter-of-factly.

And yet, he asked me all kinds of questions: "Is sound

only in specific sections of time and space? Is there no sound between the numbers on the dial?"

The fact that after the dial light had stayed on for a while, the whole thing grew warm to his touch gave rise to another set of questions. "Is sound warm?" he signed, his finger wiping imaginary sweat off his forehead. "When the radio is cold," he signed, his arms and hands shivering at his side, "is there no sound coming from it? Can there be sound in the Arctic, where it is always cold?"

I had no idea how to answer my father, but his sign was so expressive that I felt the cold. I pretended to look over my shoulder for polar bears. "Not funny," he signed, undeterred. "Is there sound everywhere down around the equator, where it's hot? Is Africa a noisy place? Alaska quiet?"

When he held his hands over the smooth dome of the radio and felt rising and falling vibrations sounding off the wood, he asked, "Does sound have rhythm? Does it rise and fall like the ocean? Does sound come and go like the wind?"

My mother, on the other hand, had no interest in the radio, how it worked, or what effect it might have on me learning to speak. She didn't waste a minute of her precious time on the whys and wherefores of the matter. She was more concerned about the everyday questions our family faced. When my father installed that giant radio in my room, my mother showed no interest. For her, the new radio was just another piece of furniture to be dusted every week, along with every other piece of furniture in our impossibly clean home.

The only questions my mother asked of me were things like, "What does the butcher man want?" and "How much is that cut of roast beef?"

These types of questions I could answer, and I felt proud and useful when I was called upon to do so. Instead of trying to explain to my father what roast beef sounded like, which I could never do in a million years, I could say, "Three dollars and fifty cents," and be rewarded with a big smile.

The radio was just the beginning of my father's questions about sound, questions that I would never quite be able to answer. After all, how do you explain sound to someone who cannot remember ever hearing it?

However, in the case of the radio, even though my

father could not hear the music coming from it, he could feel the sound it made through the soles of his feet. When he got tired of asking me questions, he would pull my mother to him, and together they would dance to the rhythm of the music rising from the wooden floor, whirling in perfect harmony around my bedroom, as smoothly as Fred Astaire and Ginger Rogers did in the movies we watched on Saturday afternoons.

I thought the musicals were horribly boring. But I loved to watch my parents dance. When they danced, it was as if they were the only two people in the world. My mother floated above the floorboards, and my father, holding her in his arms, did not have a single signed question to ask me.

CHAPTER 6

Human Telephone

By the time I was five, I had mastered enough sign and spoken English to start translating for my parents. Before long, whenever I went out with my father, I became his designated ears and mouth. This meant that he relied on me to take the silent movements of his hands and turn them into sound that others could understand. Then I had to do the process in reverse, taking the hearing person's response and turning it from invisible sound into visible sign for my father.

One day, my father took me to the poultry shop at

the corner of our block, where the chickens hung from hooks in the ceiling. His hands began to move.

"Tell Mr. Herman we want a fat chicken today," he signed, moving two fingers up and down like the beak of a pecking bird. To emphasize the size of the desired bird, he puffed out his cheeks and opened his eyes wide, as though they were bulging from the head of an enormously fat chicken. The sign was so realistic, the bird so huge, that I burst out laughing, and he laughed right along with me and exaggerated the sign.

This would be a great day, I thought. We visited the vegetable stand next.

"Mother Sarah loves corn," he signed, his fingers scraping imaginary kernels from an imaginary corncob. "But it must be fresh. Absolutely fresh." My job was to select the yellowest ears with the juiciest kernels, the plumpest red tomatoes, the heaviest potatoes, and the crispest heads of lettuce.

"Good," he signed, giving a thumbs-up. "These are perfect." He said that about everything, even the time a fat worm crawled out of a tomato I had selected with such care.

"Only a perfect tomato like this one," he had signed, "would attract such a perfect worm."

Out on the street, my father's hands told me, "Tomorrow, we will go to the zoo."

Magically, his hands turned into animals. Slowly, they swayed like an elephant's trunk. Fingers curled, they scratched his sides like a monkey. Lightly, they brushed his nose like a mouse twitching its whiskers. And his thumb peeked out from beneath the shell of his hand like a turtle's head. As I watched, my father's hands shaped the air, and I saw a zoo filled with flying birds, slithering snakes, snapping alligators, and sleek swimming seals. People stopped and looked at us. I looked only at my father's hands, imagining the fun we would have and the sights we would see.

But I was not always able to ignore people's looks. Walking home, we passed a man sitting on the curb. "I'm hungry," he whispered, his voice harsh and dry.

The man was old. His clothes were dirty. I didn't want to stop, but my father had already noticed that the man had moved his lips, so he knew he had spoken.

"What did the man say?" my father asked.

"He's hungry," I answered.

My father reached into our paper bags and pulled out some apples and a loaf of bread to give to him.

"Tell him I'm sorry," my father signed, his fist circling his heart. "But tell him things are bound to get better." My father's face lit up, showing hope, while his fingers touched his mouth, as if tasting something sweet. Good times just around the corner.

The old man asked me what was wrong with my father. "Why is he waving his hands instead of talking? What's wrong with him?"

I told him that my father was deaf.

"Tell your father I'm sorry," the man said.

Why would a homeless man feel sorry for my father? I wondered. The thought had never crossed my mind. I realized that they both felt bad for each other. Would they be willing to change places? I didn't know about the old man, but I was sure my father wouldn't. He never felt that being deaf was something to be ashamed of. And I didn't think he had a drop of self-pity in his body.

My questions would have to wait for another day. After I gave the man the food, my father took my hand,

and we continued down the street. Soon we arrived back home, and my mother was waiting by our apartment door. My father smiled, put down the paper bags, waved his arms in an excited greeting, and gathered her in his arms. There was room for me as well.

―――――――――――

Learning to speak helped me interact with my father in a new way. But it also came with great responsibility. At times, while acting as my father's human connection between sign and sound, I felt like the telephone wires strung from pole to pole through the backyards of our neighborhood. Through some unknown magic I didn't understand, these wires took sound and transformed it into something else, then sent it across huge distances, only to turn it back into perfect speech at the other end. As a deaf family, we had no telephone. I was our human telephone, missing only a dial tone. And like a telephone, I had to be available for instant use at all hours, day and night.

Mastering this unique trick of two-way communication—sound to sign, sign to sound—quickly put me in a strange position with my father. Other kids my age received mostly commands from their parents: "Do this." "Do that." "Come here." "Go there." There was no room for discussion. Whine? Up to a point. Discuss? Never.

But unlike my friends, who knew their place in the scheme of things, I had two roles. Their fathers could hear. They did not depend on their children for anything. Mine could not. And when my father was forced to interact with the hearing, he was often placed in the position of a child—ignored or dismissed. At those times, my father expected me to transform myself instantly into an adult, one who was able to speak for him, adult to adult.

Making things even more confusing, I often felt invisible during this process. It was as if I were my father's voice when I was interpreting for him. He spoke *through* me, like I was a pane of glass. Confusing as all that was, when I wasn't interpreting for my father, the roles were suddenly flipped around, and once again I was the child of my father.

One day, my father and I were in the local butcher shop. As usual on a Saturday, it was crowded. My father told me to ask the butcher for five pounds of rib roast. "Tell the butcher man, no fat!" he added firmly.

"My father wants five pounds of rib roast, no fat," I said to the butcher when we got to the head of the line.

"I'm busy, kid," he said, not even bothering to look at my father. The man knew from past experience that my father was deaf. "Tell him you'll have to wait your turn."

"What did he say?" my father asked.

"He said we have to wait our turn."

"But it is our turn. Tell the man to wait on us. Now!" my father signed, his hands plunging downward, leaving no doubt that he meant *now*! This very minute.

"My father says it's our turn now. He would like a five-pound rib roast, and no fat." I added politely, "Please, mister."

"Tell the dummy I'll say when it's his turn. Now get to the back of the line, or get out of my store."

The line of restless shoppers now stood like statues, frozen in place, staring with blank, unfeeling eyes. I felt like an animal in the zoo, imprisoned in a cage, the center of attention.

"What did the man say?" my father asked desperately. Again, I felt like a pane of glass between him and the butcher.

Part of me wanted to run, to abandon my father and escape the embarrassing spotlight he brought down on me. The other part of me wanted to stay and defend him, to explain things, and if I had to, to beg for the butcher's understanding.

But instead I froze. I stood there on the sawdust of the floor, wishing I were invisible.

"What did the man say?" my father repeated, shaking my shoulders, expecting an answer. He had taught me that I must never, ever edit what hearing people directed at him, no matter what was said. He wanted it straight. So I signed, "The man says you're a dummy," while a roaring furnace burned inside me, almost blistering my skin.

I had never heard anyone call my father a dummy before. The only time I had ever heard the word was on the radio during *The Charlie McCarthy Show* when ventriloquist Edgar Bergen called Charlie a dummy. "Charlie, you're a dummy. You're nothing but a block of wood."

My father was not a block of wood. He was no dummy. His face flushed with anger.

"Tell the man we don't want his crappy roast!" he signed with exaggerated emphasis.

"My father says, 'We'll be back, thank you.'"

Outside on the street, my father knelt down to me.

"I know you didn't tell the butcher man what I told you," he signed. "I could tell by looking at his face. That's okay. I understand. You were embarrassed. It's not fair, I know. I'm in the deaf world. You're in the hearing world.

"I need you to help me in your world. Hearing people have no time for a deaf man. No time to read my notes. They have no patience for the deaf. Hearing people think I'm stupid. I am not stupid!" My father repeatedly banged his head with a closed fist, signing, "Not stupid! Not stupid!"

My father's hands fell silent.

"No matter what they think," he finally signed to me, "I must still deal with them. So I must ask you for help. You can hear. You can speak."

My father was always so sure of himself. But now he seemed different. And I thought he might cry. I had never seen my father cry. I couldn't even imagine it. And it scared me.

Looking directly into my eyes, he slowly signed, "It

hurts me to have this need for you. You're just a boy. I hope you will understand and not hate me."

Hate my father? I was shocked. How could he think that?

"No." I shook my head.

"Never!" my hands said.

My father took me in his arms and kissed me, then held my head to his chest. I heard his heart beating.

Not long after the butcher-shop incident, my grand-mother Celia told me, "You must always take care of your parents!" That was all she said. She didn't explain herself or give me any instructions about how to follow her advice. I couldn't figure out what she meant. How could I take care of them? They were adults. And not just any adults—they were my mother and father.

But I learned.

CHAPTER 7

The Fights

Interpreting for my father occurred on the outside, in the hearing world. At home, we could communicate directly through sign. One day, though, I was called upon to perform my trick inside the walls of apartment 3A, and this time, the task required skills many light-years beyond my ability level.

It was a June night in 1938, and the occasion was a rematch between boxer Joe Louis, the man known as America's Brown Bomber, and German fighter Max Schmeling. At the time, the leader of Germany was

Adolf Hitler. He preached that Germans were a master race, and he pointed to Schmeling as one of the greatest examples of this supposed superiority. In the first match, Schmeling had knocked out Louis. Now it was time for the Brown Bomber to redeem himself and expose Hitler's lie of racial superiority.

My father came home from work that night excitedly waving the *New York Daily News*. "Look," he signed, two fingers moving from his eyes to the page. "Joe Louis is fighting Max Schmeling. Joe has *my* name." He pointed to his chest. "*L-o-u-i-s*," he finger spelled proudly.

My father was so excited about the fight that he rushed us through the dinner my mother had spent hours preparing. Normally, my father was always after me to eat slower, to chew each mouthful of food at least three times before swallowing (five times if it was calf's liver). That night, however, after gulping his food rather than chewing it, he pushed his chair away from the table and signed, "Let's go!"

By now, I had outgrown needing the radio in my bedroom. (My father was confident my ears were strong enough that I would not lose the ability to hear.) So the radio now sat prominently in the living room.

Twirling the dial, I tuned in to the broadcast. We were early. The prefight commentary detailed the career of Joe Louis, that of Schmeling, the replay of their last fight, and the significance of the rematch. I had no idea what half of the stuff meant in spoken English, much less how to translate it into sign for my father. My father didn't care. All he was interested in was the fight itself.

But that was also a problem. I knew nothing about boxing. I had never seen a match. My sport was baseball, and like every other kid in Brooklyn, I lived and died according to how well the Dodgers had done in their last game. I had no idea of exactly what went on in the boxing ring. And who were these people, anyway? Schmeling, a giant, I was told, and Louis, a black man, whose last name was my father's first name.

Questions, questions, questions. I had so many of them, but I could tell that no answers were coming, and I didn't want to let my father down. He was depending on me to tell him what happened.

By now my father had focused on me like a human microscope. I was the bug under his eye, and he looked unblinkingly at me, examining every detail, waiting to see what I would do next. We were no longer in our living room. We were ringside at Yankee Stadium.

I heard the bell ring. The crowd roared like a herd of wild beasts, the sound loud enough to wake the dead. My father just sat there, surrounded by silence, eyes locked on my hands, my face, and the radio, watching with one eye for the sound, and waiting with the other for my hands to transform the invisible, unheard sound into visible sign.

The fight was on. The noise of the crowd and the screaming voice of the announcer poured out in a torrent of sound. I tried to sign what was happening, to keep up with what I was hearing. But there was just too much noise coming at me, all crowded together. Besides, my signing vocabulary did not include signs for the boxing game. Oh sure, I could sign *chicken*. That was easy, as the sign *looked* like a chicken. I could sign *corn*. (I was great with vegetables. My father had taught me a garden of signs—a whole *farm* full of signs.)

But how was I supposed to sign, *The Brown Bomber lands with an uppercut. Now he's jabbing Schmeling. Jab, jab, jab. There's no letup. Schmeling's eye is closing. Jab, jab, another jab to the eye. Joe Louis is killing him. Another uppercut. One to the breadbasket. Schmeling doubles over. Ooohh, that one will bring up his lunch.*

Pained frustration pinched my father's face as he tried to make sense of my incomprehensible, stuttering signs.

Equally frustrated, I leaped instinctively to my feet, swinging my arms, my fists extended. As I listened to each detail describing the action in the ring, I danced in circles in front of my father. I swung. I ducked. I bobbed. I weaved—imagining what I was hearing.

The punches I threw jolted my arms. The invisible impact of their landing shot up into my shoulders. I hunched in pain. But my face was Joe Louis's determined mask, the one my father had shown me in the newspaper. I was killing Schmeling. Take *that*! How about *this*! Smack, my leather glove beat down on Schmeling's face. So much for the master race, I thought.

I rose on my toes and went after the retreating, cowering Schmeling. I heard the announcer scream, *He can run, but he can't hide. Louis has Schmeling on the ropes. He's pounding away at him. HE'S DOWN! HE'S DOWN! SCHMELING'S DOWN! He's on the canvas.*

I dropped to the floor and lay spread-eagle on the rag rug.

Louis is standing over Schmeling.

I jumped up, staring down at the rug.

Schmeling's twitching.

I drop to the floor. Roll on my back. I twitch.

Schmeling's as still as a stone.

I lay still as a stone.

The referee waves Louis to a neutral corner.

I jumped up and follow his command, taking myself to what I decided was the neutral corner of the room.

ONE.

I sign with exaggerated emphasis the number one... *TWO*...two...*THREE*...three...*Schmeling's trying to get up*...I fell down. I tried to rise...and continue signing... *FOUR*...four...*FIVE*...five...*Schmeling falls back to the canvas*...I fall back on the rug...*SIX*...six...I sign the number from the floor...*SEVEN*...seven...*EIGHT*... eight...*NINE*...nine...*TEN*...I make a fist, thrust my thumb up, and wiggle my hand furiously...TEN.

It's all over! Schmeling's out! I'm signing like a maniac. *The Brown Bomber is the Heavyweight Champion of the W.O.R.L.D!*

The noise from my radio was deafening.

I paraded around the room, arms raised in victory. The cheering pouring from the radio was music to my ears. "Take *that*, Adolf," I shouted at the top of my lungs. My father whooped and hollered and stamped his feet on the floor in wild, unleashed joy.

The neighbors in the apartment below us began pounding on their ceiling with the end of a broom. Our next-door neighbors began banging on the wall between our apartments with shoes. The neighbors upstairs were stomping their feet on their floor. It was chaos. My mother felt the noise from the floor below her feet, and the vibrations from the walls and ceiling, and ran into the room in a panic.

My father heard nothing, but the look on his face said it all. He was laughing uncontrollably at my performance. Tears streamed out of his eyes and ran down his cheeks.

"Great fight!" he signed when he caught his breath. "I understood everything!"

I stood there in the middle of the ring, on the rag-rug canvas, exhausted but proud. Thank goodness, I thought, the fight had lasted less than one round. I was in no shape to go the distance.

CHAPTER 8

Another Child

When I was four, my family welcomed a new addition to our silent world.

My brother, Irwin, was born hearing, like me. (In fact, about 90 percent of children born to deaf parents can hear.) When it was announced at the hospital that the new baby could hear, it was assumed by both sides of the family that the "curse of deafness" had been broken. With this baby, there were no regularly scheduled weekend visits for family to come to our apartment for the yearlong ritual of banging on pots and pans.

From the day my mother came home from the hospital, I became my brother's third parent. No longer did my mother have to rely on tying a ribbon from her arm to her new baby's foot. That velvet ribbon had been replaced by me. And as far as my mother was concerned, I was a much better connection between her newborn son and herself. After all, a ribbon can't speak in sign. Just as I was my father's connection to the outside world, I became my mother's connection to her second son.

My brother's crib was placed next to my bed. And when he awoke at night crying for his bottle, it was my job to wake my mother. When he awoke at night with a stomachache, it was my job to wake my mother. When he awoke at night, fussy and restless, it was my job to wake my mother. But as he grew, he would sometimes wake up just because he was no longer sleepy. Then I would play with him as he lay on his back in his crib.

My brother was an extremely happy baby, somewhat on the chubby side. He was quick to make eye contact and just as quick to smile and giggle. When I looked at him, he looked right back at me and cycled his legs and waved his arms in excitement. I would wave my arms back at him to see if I could get an even bigger response. And when this didn't work, I would make faces at him.

Having learned from my parents the exaggerated facial expressions and body language that are a part of the grammar of sign language, I would sign to my baby brother every morning when he awoke to a new day, "I am so very happy to see you." I always exaggerated the hand sign for *happy* by striking my chest over my heart with the open palm of my hand—to awaken my heart to a throbbing happiness at the sight of him. As a conductor would lead a fifty-piece orchestra in wild abandon, my palms hit and bounced off my chest, my arms windmilling, while I raised my eyebrows high in shock and amazement, and I ballooned my cheeks to bursting to see if he would imitate me. My performance was almost always rewarded by my brother's expression of wild delight, and his flailing arms and kicking legs attempting to mirror my physical craziness.

There were other times—in the middle of the night—that I thought to teach my brother to speak.

Who knows? I wondered. If I could teach him to speak well, maybe he could one day take my place as the translator for my father.

Also, I thought it would be nice to have someone I could talk to. After all, although voices were constantly spilling from the speakers in our living room, I couldn't hold a conversation with the radio.

I was curious about what my brother's speaking voice would sound like. Living with my parents, whose spoken words sounded harsh, I was used to listening to the sound of speech—pronounced words, their accents, and, in the case of my friend Jerry's Italian father, the music of their speech. And so, as my brother looked up at me— wide awake, and not in the least bit sleepy—I looked down at him and repeated words over and over again, hoping to get a response.

Of course, for a while, none came. But I was determined to be the human replacement for the radio that spoke to me when I was a baby. And after a while, at an unusually early age, he did begin to speak. I couldn't believe I had succeeded. It was as if I had performed some kind of magic trick.

As he grew, I continued to talk to Irwin, and he lay in his crib, studying my face and lips. Slowly but surely, he learned bigger and more difficult words—words whose meaning he had no idea of.

My plan was working, and I was sure that I would eventually have a hearing and talking friend in my brother. But that was not to be.

One shocking night when I was nine years old, my relationship with my brother changed forever. That night I awoke to sounds I had never heard before. I groped for the switch on my bedside lamp, and when I turned the knob, the sight of my brother took my breath away. In the bed next to mine, where he had slept all his life, my brother was laying as rigid as a plank of wood.

As I watched, his brown eyes rolled back in his head so that only the whites were showing. His mouth was clamped shut, biting down on his tongue and spurting blood all over his white pillowcase. His body squirmed and writhed and jerked about. His arms and legs flew in every direction, like the flailing arms of a windmill. Sweat was flying from his body. I was stunned, turned to stone.

I don't know if his convulsions lasted one minute or an hour. Time had no meaning. My entire focus was on my brother as he was transformed into a creature I could not understand.

When he was finally still, which happened, it seemed, in an instant, he lay there drenched in sweat, his face covered in blood, completely unconscious.

In time—I can't say how long—I rushed to get my father and mother. When I jolted my father awake, the look on my face threw him into a panic, and my mother screamed. No signs were necessary. My face said it all. Rushing into my bedroom, they saw a sight that must have been the stuff of their nightmares: their son covered in blood, blood everywhere on his sheets and pillow, while he lay barely breathing.

While my mother held him in her arms, my father wiped the blood from his body and face with a damp cloth, searching for its source.

That evening was the beginning of a year of nonstop nightly seizures, which involved a sudden surge of electricity in his brain, a loss of consciousness, and the start of violent shaking of every part of his body. Our family doctor explained the situation to me while my parents looked on, waiting helplessly for me to translate the doctor's words. He told me my little brother had epilepsy.

"Why?" my father signed angrily. "Why?" he demanded over and over again. "Isn't it enough that we are deaf?"

I did not know what to tell my father. Neither did the doctor. After I made it clear to him that my brother had not been sick, nor had he fallen and hit his head, and that no one else in our entire family had ever had a seizure, his only comment was, "Tell your father that I have no answer for him. These things happen in the brain. It's like a short circuit."

That did not satisfy my father. "Idiot!" he signed.

"What did your father say?" the doctor asked me.

Here we go, I thought. I did not want to offend the doctor, and I didn't want to embarrass myself, but at the same time, I did not want to be disrespectful to my father. So, like other times, I translated my father's sign into "Thank you."

After my brother's first episode, every night when we went to bed, my father tied a cloth strip from my arm to my brother's arm. On my bedside table was a selection of wooden tongue depressors, which my father had covered in thick gauze.

My instructions were simple. "When you feel the cloth jerk, that's the signal that Irwin will be going into a seizure. Get up immediately. Straddle your brother, force his jaws open, clear his tongue away from his teeth, and slip the tongue depressor between his jaws, making sure, doubly sure, that his tongue is clear of his teeth. Then, and only then, remove your fingers from his mouth. Be sure, but be quick. When he goes into convulsions, hold him as still as you can. Whatever you do, don't let him jerk himself off of his bed." He added, "Your mother and I are counting on you. You can hear. We are deaf."

Over time, I became quite good at these peculiar skills. I began to sleep lightly, never dreaming, and would snap awake the instant my brother stiffened, which happened each night that first year, as regular as an alarm clock. His arm would jerk, the cloth between us would yank my arm, and I would leap onto his body, straddling him between my thighs. A gauze-wrapped tongue depressor found its way into my hand without any thought on my part. Holding his mouth open, I thrust the depressor into his mouth and pushed aside his tongue.

Most nights I was successful. Some nights, I got my fingers out of his mouth before it snapped shut but was not able to clear his tongue completely from his biting jaws. Then the blood would fly. Other nights, I was not quick enough to remove my fingers before his jaws clamped shut, and my blood would mix with his.

Deep into that year, my brother began to have episodes of repeated seizures. When this happened, I had to wake our downstairs neighbor and ask to use her phone so that I could call for an ambulance. She did not complain once. When the ambulance arrived, I accompanied my father and my unconscious brother to Coney Island Hospital. There I went through the usual routine of being my father's ears and voice. But this time, I was also the voice and ears of my unconscious brother.

As Irwin grew older, I was tasked not only with teaching him how to speak, but also with being the translator between him and our parents. In time, he gained basic skills in sign language from casual instruction from our parents. But for much of our childhood, he relied on me to translate the more complex flow of signs directed at him. My first language had been sign. Now, because of me, my brother's first language would be spoken, and I would have to translate between him and our parents.

There were times when I became angry about my situation. It was one thing to be singled out on my street as the son of the "deafies in 3A," which is all my parents were ever known as on our block. Not Louis and Sarah. Not Mr. and Mrs. Uhlberg. But the "deaf and dumb mutes in 3A." This I had gotten used to.

But to be "minding" my brother in the street on a sunny afternoon when my father was at work and my mother was cleaning our apartment and to have him suddenly stiffen and fall to the pavement was another thing entirely. His body would go rigid, as if petrified, transformed in an instant into a stony replica of my brother.

My friends would swarm around us, staring openmouthed at the sight of Irwin thrashing uncontrollably on the sidewalk, often sliding off the curb and into the gutter. All the while I was on top of him, as if riding a bucking horse.

To make things worse, my mother somehow always seemed to sense what was happening. She would stop what she was doing, lean out the window, and begin wailing at the sight.

Why was I the only kid on my block—certainly in all of Brooklyn, probably in the entire world—who was responsible for an epileptic brother and two deaf parents? I wondered, feeling sorry for myself. Why couldn't I be like everyone else on my block? It just wasn't fair. I was just a kid.

CHAPTER 9

Heaven

When looking after my brother and translating for my father became too much for me, I escaped to the roof of my apartment building.

The roof was my personal sanctuary, my heaven. On summer days, I sat in silence, my back to the low, warm brick wall that edged the roof, with nothing but blue sky above my head. On that roof, on such a day, my ears were not filled with the constant noises of my Brooklyn block, and my eyes were not filled with the signs of my father or the image of my brother suddenly stiffening and dropping to the ground.

I read every copy of my comic-book collection, over and over again. I got lost in the adventures—the close calls, the speeding trains, the angry lions, the nefarious crooks—and dreamed that my life was normal, as it was for the other kids on my block whose parents could hear.

The roof wasn't just my own, of course. On summer evenings, the neighbors gathered there to cool off, sitting in family groups on blankets spread over the graveled tar paper, covered edge to edge with cold chicken, lemonade, potato salads, and cakes and cookies. I migrated with the rest of the kids from blanket to blanket, trying a cookie or a drumstick for no other reason than to see if somebody else's food tasted any different from my mother's efforts.

Tuesday nights in summer were particularly special. As the sky darkened over Coney Island, fireworks shot up—banging, crackling, humming, and whistling—into the sky over the Atlantic, where they burst into a bloom of light against the purple horizon. On rooftops all over my neighborhood, collective oohs and aahs rose to the sky in a chorus of appreciation.

I was happy for the noise. It meant that my father's

harsh voice blended in with everyone else's, and no one stared at us. And my little brother sat mercifully still, watching with open mouth and eyes wide open, nodding along with each new explosion.

But the roof was more than just a place for watching fireworks. It was also the highest spot on my block, and I soon took to keeping watch over our neighborhood.

It was 1942, and World War II was in full swing. Adolf Hitler's army had conquered almost all of Europe. And I knew the German soldiers would want to attack the United States next. Fortunately, there was an ocean between them and us. But they might try to get to us by airplane, I imagined.

When the weather was clear, I went up to the roof with my official enemy-plane-spotter cards. This was my deck of playing cards with the silhouettes of German aircraft illustrated on them. I knelt behind the brick wall with my father's binoculars, so I would not be seen by the enemy pilots, and I looked to the east over Coney Island, the direction Hitler's planes would surely come from. Why they would come to Brooklyn was never a question that entered my mind. Perhaps to bomb Nathan's Famous hot dog stand, whose food kept up the spirits of every person in Brooklyn. I knew that the loss of their franks and buttered popcorn would be a near-mortal blow.

But my roof was not just a summer place.

In the winter, after a heavy snowfall, when the rest of the kids ran down into the street, I would go in the other direction. It was a challenge to push the roof door open against the piled-up snow, but once it was accomplished, I had the place all to myself. I spent hours trekking through the snow, my footprints the only ones disturbing its smooth surface.

When enough snow had fallen, I made enormous snowballs. They were cannonball size. Then bomb size. These I lobbed over the wall onto the unsuspecting neighbors below. I was not the bombardier of a B-17, Flying Fortress, and I had no bombsight instrument, but my accuracy was outstanding.

My trips to the roof never helped prevent an attack by Nazi bombers—because no such attack ever came. And I'm sure my neighbors grew tired of dodging my snow bombs as they plummeted to the sidewalk, but the roof gave me something I couldn't find anywhere else. A place to be myself.

CHAPTER 10

Clothes Make the Boy

My father was determined for me to have a "normal" childhood despite the differences in our home life from other families on the block. And so, every summer, about a month before the beginning of the school year, he set in motion an annual ritual. And once started, it was my signal that summer was over. Oh sure, the calendar on my wall still said *July*, but this day proved that the calendar was lying. I could almost feel the chill of autumn on my bare skin.

The curtain opened on this yearly production with my father's hands shaking me awake. "School starts thirty days from now!" they said, practically screaming at me. "There's a big sale on boys' suits at Mr. R. and H. Macy's store today. We must hurry!"

My father had not owned a single suit as a boy. But he insisted that I needed a new one every year to help me fit in. The thing was, I didn't know a single other kid whose father insisted on getting him a suit every year. And shopping with my father was far from a normal experience.

"Time is short. Hurry! Hurry!" he signed with insistent, choppy movements. "We've got to get a move on before all the good stuff is snapped up."

"Good stuff? Snapped up?" I said under my breath. Of course, I didn't have to mumble, but I did have to be careful, because my father could read my lips.

Slowly, I dragged myself out of bed. I was in no rush to begin this day. A day that would bring me no joy. A day that was sure to be wall-to-wall embarrassment as I played the go-between, negotiating the sale of a suit with my father on one side and a bunch of unsympathetic, impatient hearing salesmen on the other. To make matters worse, the salesmen worked on commission. They were paid based on how much they could sell, so for them, time was money. My father, on the other hand, had all the time in the world.

"We'll start with Mr. Bloomingdale," my father's hands informed me. "His basement has a ton of suits. All with two pants. And he has the best prices in the city."

Best prices? I thought. Sure, but in all the time we've shopped there, we've never bought a single suit. Bloomingdale's basement was just that, the starting point in an endless day.

"Who knows," my father added. "If we're lucky, we'll find a two-for-one sale."

After two subway rides that took us from the far reaches of Brooklyn to the treeless streets of Manhattan, we exited into a different world. Lexington Avenue was already clogged with trucks and cabs, and as my father took my hand and we marched across the crosswalk, sweaty, angry-looking drivers honked impatiently and yelled words that luckily my father could not hear.

When we reached the other side, my father dropped my hand, and now freed from my grasp, his hands flung excitement in every direction. "What a great day this is! Me with my son Myron, out to buy a suit. A *beautiful* day. Listen! Can you hear the sunshine sound on the lady's red dress in the window? And look at the light of the sunshine. See how it breaks up into diamonds in the puddle at the curb. Smell the exhaust from the automobiles. Can you taste it on the back of your tongue?"

My father often said things like this. It was like all his other senses were heightened to make up for the loss of his hearing. He even claimed to "hear" the sound of color, which didn't make any sense to me.

Leaving the sunlit street, we descended into the artificial light of Bloomingdale's basement. That's where the two-for-one suits were located. And there were thousands of them hanging in a huge, poorly lit room. I could swear my father licked his lips at the sight of all the wool.

He always began by instructing me to try on the suits that were sewn of the heaviest wool fabrics. Pattern didn't matter: plaids, stripes, herringbone. Weave was not an issue: serge, gabardine, worsted. Price was of no concern. Nothing mattered except sheer weight. He wanted to buy me a suit that would last.

"These are great," his hands assured me, while his face accompanied his happy hands with a big, satisfied smile. "These are bulletproof suits."

"Great," my hands said doubtfully. "These suits would serve me well in the invasion of Europe. What German soldier would shoot at a kid from Brooklyn wearing a plaid suit like this? And if he did, how surprised he'd be when the bullets bounced off the lapels."

I could tell by my father's expression he didn't think my joke was funny. His response was, "Follow me."

Off to the dressing room we went, my father with ten wool suits clutched to his chest, me following reluctantly behind. The way his arms drooped, I figured the suits must have weighed a hundred pounds.

"Where is a salesman?" my father signed in the suddenly deserted room. "They're never around when you need one."

I didn't have the heart to tell him that at the sight of us, every salesman in the place had scurried off about as fast as the cockroaches in our kitchen did when I turned on the light in the middle of the night. Our fruitless, salesless annual visits had not been forgotten by those who worked on commission. Every summer, in came my father, and off ran the salesmen.

"Never mind," my father signed. "I know Mr. Bloomingdale's inventory like I know the contents of my closet. It never changes."

Suit after suit I tried on. Modeling each one for my father while being rotated by him, like a chicken on a spit, I stood in front of a huge, tilted floor mirror.

"Not right," he said. "Bunches up in the back. Makes you look like a little hunchback man. The same as in that sad movie. You know, the man who rings the church bell. Try this one next.

"Too tight. Try the next one.

"Plaid makes you look fat, like the man in the circus." He laughed at the thought, but I did not join in his hilarity. Actually, by now I felt like crying.

"Try this one.

"The stripes make you look like a string-bean boy. Green suit makes you look good enough to eat. Like a vegetable. Maybe we'll take you home and Mother Sarah will cook our son Myron in his new green string-bean suit."

Oh, what a day this would be.

"Try this one on next."

Suit after itchy wool suit I tried on and modeled for my father.

None were satisfactory to his eye.

Hours passed. Suit after suit was plucked off the rack and brought to me in the dressing room. Suit after suit took its place on the dressing room wall, then the dressing room bench, and finally, stacked up neatly on the dressing room floor.

When my father had tried every single suit in my size, as well as sizes I could never grow into before they went out of style—if they had ever been in style—he threw up his hands, announcing, "Well, that's it for Mr. Bloomingdale. He had his chance. We gave him first crack."

"But we never *ever* buy a suit from Bloomingdale's," I pointed out to my father. "We come here every year. I try on every suit they have in my size, even sizes too large for me. 'You'll grow into this someday,' you say. And after all those solids and plaids and stripes and herringbones, you always say, 'Well, that's it for Mr. Bloomingdale.'"

"Quality," my father signed patiently, as if explaining

to a backward child. "That's what we're after. Only the very best suit is good enough for my son Myron."

"Who's this Myron fellow?" I wondered. It always threw me for a loop when my father would suddenly use my name as if I were not in the room right next to him. There we were, I pictured in my mind—my father and this guy, Myron, and me.

Holding my hand in his left hand while signing abbreviated signs with his right, my father launched us back into the stream of traffic on Lexington Avenue.

"Next stop, Mr. R. and H. Macy. Largest store in the world." I looked at the expansiveness of my father's sign as his hands spread wide describing the size of R. H. Macy & Co., and my heart dropped at the mere thought of the visit.

Safely on the other side of the avenue—after my father had stared down a fast-approaching taxi, daring it hit us—we boarded a bus, then ducked into the subway for a short ride downtown. Climbing out of the station at Thirty-Fourth Street, we stood at the entrance to the home of R. H. Macy & Co. An enormous place, it took up an entire square block, street to street, avenue to avenue. I couldn't begin to imagine how many suits in my size it might contain. I wondered if Mr. R. and H. Macy kept his store open twenty-four hours a day, seven days a week. There was no way we could get through all the suits in this place before school started.

With a look of fierce determination on his face, my father took my hand. We whirled through the giant revolving door and, with a score of other shoppers, were swept into a waiting elevator, which rose with sudden, stomach-dropping acceleration, quickly dumping us into the middle of the suit department.

Spread out before us was a vast ocean of suits, row upon endless row, quite possibly all the suits that had ever been made. The thought of the total number of sheep that had been clipped to produce the wool that had been woven into the cloth that was used to make these endless flocks of suits staggered my imagination. I imagined all those poor, cold, shivering sheep huddled together on a grassy hill in Scotland, trying to stay warm.

I glanced up at my father and saw a look of pure happiness spread across his face. Taking a firm grip on my hand, his face now set in determination, my father waded bravely into the oncoming waves of hanging suits, stretching out to the horizon of elevators, with me following in his wake.

Now the second act of this dreadful play began—and this would also be a long one, as Mr. R. and H. Macy had, if possible, even more suits than Mr. Bloomingdale—and apparently even fewer salesmen, for the clothing salesmen in Macy's saw my father coming and ran even faster for cover.

When we finally returned to our neighborhood at the end of our epic day together, the third act of the drama began. As we exited the Sea Beach line subway stop at Kings Highway, my father signed, "You've been a good boy today. I'm proud of you. You were a big help to me. And you were fun company. Now for your reward."

Our neighborhood candy store was our source not only for candy but also other delights, some of them ordinary, some strange. It was where we bought our brand-new Spaldeen rubber balls, which we smacked around the street with a sawed-off broomstick in our pickup baseball games. And when we had the money, we bought a variety of delicious things to eat: chocolate kisses in their silver wrappers or button candy dripped as dots onto tissue paper (which were great until you got bits of paper stuck between your teeth). There were also ridiculous items for sale, like ruby-red wax lips, which were perfectly molded into the shape of a smile but were about as flavorful as mud. With these fat, red lips clenched firmly between our front teeth, we would parade around the neighborhood, pressing our faces into the thighs of every grown-up we encountered, pretending we were vampires out to drink their blood.

"Choose anything you want," my father signed. "Even two things today."

I didn't know where to begin.

As always, my father was patient. "Take your time," he said. So in imitation of him in the department stores, I ever-so-carefully examined every comic book in the store, handled every small toy, and fingered every small trinket—just as he had examined every wool suit hanging on the pipe racks at Mr. Bloomingdale's and Mr. R. and H. Macy's. Finally, I settled on a Batman comic and a set of wax lips.

"I'll wear them when we get home," I told him. "Mother won't recognize me." My father smiled at the image of me walking through our front door grinning like an idiot with my ruby-red lips.

"Can we get a set for Irwin?" I asked. "That way, Mother will be doubly surprised."

Readily agreeing, my father, like the great director he was, staged the conclusion of the final act: egg cream sodas for both of us—and so the curtain came down. The play was over. I had my new suit. My father had had his day alone with his son. And in his eyes, we were no different from the other so-called "normal" families on the street.

CHAPTER 11

A Day in the City

I had never gotten closer to where my father worked than the feeling of wearing a newspaper hat, which he'd make from the paper he brought home every evening. But one day just after I turned nine years old, my father, who had the day off, took me to the *Daily News* Building. I had heard all about his work, and I knew how proud he was of his job. Now it was time to see it all behind the scenes.

That morning, he selected the clothes I would wear—beginning with that year's new suit, of course. Then he put on his best clothes and freshly polished shoes. After kissing my mother and brother goodbye, we went down into the street and walked to the Kings Highway stop on the BMT subway, where we went down the stairs and stood on the platform for the train to Manhattan.

The train took us into the city, where we transferred to another train, which took us to a stop near my father's workplace. Exiting the subway, my father took my hand and urged me to walk faster. Soon, we arrived in front of the *Daily News* Building.

I stood with my father outside the glass-covered entrance to the lobby. No matter how far backward I bent, I simply could not see the top of the building. The rows of vertical white-brick panels rose from the city sidewalk straight up into a limitless blue sky, where they seemed to merge into a single point, thirty-seven floors above my head. Big, white clouds looked like fat dirigibles sailing slowly overhead, preparing to dock on the roof.

Pushing our way through the revolving door, we entered the splendor of the high-domed lobby of the *Daily News* Building. I had never seen anything like it. The space was dark, lit only in strategic places. The floor we stood on was made of slick squares. And there in front of me, sitting halfway down a wide, deep hole, behind a railing, revolved an enormous globe.

It was a single, endlessly spinning object bathed in light in the otherwise dark lobby. Every known country was outlined in bright colors. Every city noted. The seven blue oceans divided the continents. The North Pole whitely capped the top, while its distant relative, the South Pole, completed the picture deep down in the well.

As I stared in amazement, I began to wonder where my block was. And for that matter, where was Brooklyn? How big would the ball need to be to show West Ninth Street? At least the size of the Wonder Wheel on Coney Island. And the lobby that housed such a globe would have to be the size of…what? I simply couldn't imagine. As for the size of the building that could house the lobby that contained a globe the size of the Wonder Wheel, it was beyond the outer limit of even my wildest imagination.

"Nice," I signed.

After I had seen enough of the lobby, we rode the elevator, going up in a stomach-dropping *whoosh* to the floor where my father worked. The elevator car stopped with a suddenness that threatened to bring up my breakfast.

From the moment we left the quiet of the elevator and stepped onto the printing-press floor, we penetrated the wall of sound so deafening that I could not hear myself think. In the enormous press room, seven printing presses, each as big as a two-story house, were pounding away, printing sixty-thousand copies of the *Daily News* an hour. These vast, two-storied machines were a mind-boggling collection of wheels, struts, rollers, and chains. Into one end, giant rolls of blank white paper ran, eventually to be spat out in the form of finished newsprint at the other end.

No matter how far I stuffed my fingers into my ears, I could not shut out the sound. And the sound was not just in my ears. The thundering rumble that rose from the wood and concrete floor went straight up my legs and through my spine. I imagined this was what it would be like to stand on an African plain, with a thousand elephants running past me, scared for their lives.

My father led me from workstation to workstation, showing me off to each of his coworkers. When the presses were running, the deaf pressmen wore newspaper hats on their hair (to protect from the mist of ink that rose off the presses) and smiles of a job well done on their faces.

Their hearing coworkers, cotton wadding plugged into their ears, wore matching newspaper hats on their heads, but pained expressions on their faces. Now I understood why my father and his deaf coworkers had been hired by the boss, Captain Patterson. Being deaf was an advantage in these work conditions. The noise did not distract them from performing their tasks, as it did the hearing workers.

When the presses shuddered to a stop, as the last copy of the day's newspaper came down the conveyor belt, my father waved goodbye to his coworkers in the pressroom and marched me off to the composing room, where he worked. This huge space housed row upon row upon row of men working at typesetting machines, each with a keyboard that looked as if it belonged to a typewriter. But instead of typing onto a sheet of paper, the machines produced letters and words encased in blocks of metal.

Here was a different sound. Unlike the rolling rumble of panicked elephants in the pressroom, the composing room was filled with the clanging of metal on metal. It reminded me of a jungle crowded with screeching monkeys. Back into my ears went my fingers.

Other workers stood shoulder to shoulder, their nimble

fingers taking out lead-font type from waist-high metal cases and placing them skillfully into steel frames. The workers were taking news articles that had been written by reporters and putting them into lead type. It was this type that would later be stamped onto the pages by the printing presses. When a "page" had been completed in the steel frame, the whole thing was locked into place with a metal key.

This was where my father stood five days a week. Hunched over his workstation, eyeshades protecting his eyes from the glare of fluorescent lights. Pushing me in front of him, he led me forward to meet his deaf coworkers, who immediately stopped their work and greeted me, each trying to get my attention with large, exaggerated signs.

My father told me later that his deaf friends were comparing my signing ability with that of their own children. He told me I had done well in their eyes, as some had children who didn't sign very well. This was usually the case with the second child, because that child was not required to be the family interpreter. The exception, he explained, was when the second child was a girl, as girls tended to be better signers that boys. (My father told my mother that night, when he recapped the day for her, that I had received a great compliment from his pals—that I signed like a girl. Seeing my father's hands sign "same as a girl," my brother laughed out loud. I, on the other hand, found no humor in the compliment.)

Meeting my father's hearing coworkers was a much different experience. These men had never once exchanged a meaningful sentence with my father in all the years they had stood side by side in the composing room. I made sure to shake everyone's hand, but some of the comments I heard when I removed my fingers from my ears upset me.

To my face, the men said, "Nice to meet you kid. How come you can hear?" And, "How do you like having a deaf father?" "Why does your father talk funny?" "Did your father ever go to school?" And one man even asked me, "Did your father become deaf because his mother dropped him on his head?" He wasn't kidding.

My father did not notice these questions. He proudly beamed down on me as he saw my hand engulfed in the large hands of his "pals." And that was bad enough, as far as I was concerned.

But what I heard when we walked away was even more shocking. The men spoke behind our backs as though I too was unable to hear. "Look at the dummy's kid. He looks normal." "Lou has a nice-looking kid. I wonder why." "Hey, look at that, the dummy's kid. He can talk good." "Would you believe it? The dummy has a kid who can talk." I couldn't believe what they were saying, but I managed to hide my surprise from my father.

I found out later that I didn't need to. My father knew exactly what his hearing coworkers thought and said about him behind his back. But on that day in the *Daily News* Building, he showed no sign of it. His face registered only pride—about his work and about having me there, his hearing son.

My father's deafness often made things hard. From the minute we stepped out of our home and entered the hearing world together, it felt as though we were going into battle. And I often felt outnumbered in the conflicts that came our way. But as I watched my father walk away from the uninformed, cruel questions of his coworkers, I saw that he was strong. And I knew he wouldn't give an inch. He would always stand his ground.

I wasn't always sure that I could.

PART II

West Ninth Street

CHAPTER 12

The Sound of Color

My parents were the only deaf people in our neighborhood, and because of this, we did not often have visitors to our apartment. But this did not mean my parents didn't socialize. The beach on Coney Island was where the deaf people from across New York City came to be with each other during the summer months—to visit, to argue, to share the latest jokes, for the singles to flirt, for the married to complain, and for everyone to catch up on the latest deaf community news and the news about the Depression. It was like a great, big deaf outdoor living room.

One Sunday in the middle of August, my father and I were walking along Surf Avenue on our way to the beach on Coney Island. Above us, gray storm clouds were gathering. Where they came together, the gray blended into black. And where they piled up, one massive black cloud upon another, they turned an even darker shade of black. A cold, salty breeze suddenly swept down Surf Avenue from the direction of Nathan's Famous hot dog stand, loaded with the blended smells of grilled franks and mustard, knishes, hot buttered corn, and a whiff of popcorn.

Day turned into night as lightning split the darkness, followed by claps of thunder. The clouds cracked open, and rain tumbled from the sky, quickly turning the steaming asphalt into small rivers carrying Coney Island debris on their backs. The storm drains backed up, causing miniature waves to break across Surf Avenue. The rides in the amusement park emptied and stopped. People ran for cover as the rain fell in wind-driven sheets of water. I tugged on my father's hand, but he stood still, looking up at the blackest sky I had ever seen.

"What does black sound like?" he asked me.

It was not exactly the best time to answer my father's impossible questions about sound. Thunder loud enough to hurt my ears banged down on my head.

"Like thunder," I signed, repeatedly banging my two fists together.

"I don't understand," he signed, his face pinched in frustration. "What does thunder sound like?"

I was desperate. I was soaked. I began to shiver. "Like a hammer," I signed, now raising and lowering my fist, as if I were striking my opposite fist with an invisible hammer. My father thought about that, his face relaxing into comprehension. "Yes, like a hammer. Hard, like my hands."

Satisfied, he took my hand, and we ran under an awning. The small trees along the curb bent in the wind. Leaves torn from their thin branches flew all around us.

"I feel the wind on my face. Tell me, what is the wind's sound?" my father asked.

I felt the wind on my face as well. I began to be afraid that out in the open, we might be struck by lightning. And I realized that the flimsy awning we stood under would be no protection at all. Yet here my father was, asking me to explain the sound of the wind.

As I was thinking of an answer, the black clouds blew out over the ocean. The Wonder Wheel began to turn, the empty white cars swinging out over the boardwalk, reflecting golden sunlight. The sun shone down. The storm had passed.

"Never mind," my father signed. "We'll go to the beach before all the good spots are taken." My mother was home with a cold that day, with my brother for company. "Say hi to the deafies," she had told me as we went out the door that morning.

We were not the first to arrive at the patch of beach that had long ago been claimed by the deaf as their own, the place where they could all be together. Three deaf couples from the Bronx and one from Queens had gotten there before us. They always did, since they did not want to have to sit on the warmer, boardwalk side of the circle that would form and re-form all day long with each new arrival. We added our beach chairs to the circle, which immediately expanded to let us in.

All morning long, the deaf came from every borough in New York City. With each new arrival, conversations stopped in midair while chairs were lifted and readjusted to enlarge the circle. Then the hands resumed their flight in midsentence, gesturing furiously to one another. I was always amazed by the wild diversity of language on display.

The men tended to sign more aggressively, more assertively than the women. The outgoing personalities signed expansively, while the shy tended to make smaller, more guarded signs. Some signed with abandon, even boisterously, while others signed hesitantly. Some signed loudly, some softly. Some signed with comic exaggeration, while the signing of others was controlled and thoughtful. A couple who had moved to the Bronx from a small town in Georgia signed with an accent I didn't recognize. My father told me they signed with a drawl, and as I watched, I could see that their signs did seem to flow from their hands like syrup, thick and slow.

There was one deaf lady who had suffered a stroke many years before who seemed to stutter when she signed. It was as though her signs stuck to her hands. Impatiently, she shook them off her fingers in an attempt to be understood.

One man's signs seemed halting, primitive, even childish. My father caught me staring, a puzzled look on my face, and explained.

"When he was a boy, he lived on a farm. He grew up deaf on that farm. He had a big hearing family, but his family had no sign. His family was poor. It was a hard life. His father needed the boy to help with the farmwork. Finally, the boy went to deaf school when he was fourteen years old. There he learned sign. But it was too late. He never learned good. He is still a little deaf boy in his own mind. Now all the time he talks like a child. Simple. He never gets better. Sad."

My father's signs tended to be quick, impatient, insistent. This was typical of the signs of the deaf who lived in a big city.

As I looked out over all those hands shaping word pictures painted in the air above the sand of Coney Island, the scene seemed as action packed, and as colorful, as a picture I saw in a book of the ceiling above the Sistine Chapel.

More deaf couples arrived, lugging beach chairs and picnic baskets and beach umbrellas, their kids hanging on for dear life. The circle readjusted to welcome the newcomers. Down went the beach chairs and up went the hands, fluttering wildly like the wings of a flock of geese taking flight. They had not seen each other since last weekend, and there was much news to tell.

Rushing over the hot sand, we joined the group. My father set up his beach chair around the perimeter. I sat with the other kids on beach towels in the middle of the ever-expanding circle, like small animals in a human cage made up of our parents, beach chairs, and beach umbrellas, our protection against the possibility of getting lost.

It was always a strange feeling being with a large group of deaf people. I was used to being in public with my parents. But here I was just one kid among many. I felt safe in this group.

Still, I found myself wondering how we must look to the hearing people outside our circle. I knew they would assume that we were all deaf. After all, we all spoke with our hands instead of our mouths. Even the hearing kids. It would not be polite if we spoke, rather than signed.

Overhead, a flock of seagulls flew across the sky. I imagined what we all must look like to them, packed together, arms waving like windmills, while around us, scattered folks sat on individual blankets, gawking at us. Whenever I was in public with my parents, I felt the eyes of the hearing watching. But I knew the sea gulls wouldn't care one way or the other. To them we were all the same. And since they had no ears, I wasn't even sure if they could hear.

Still, I daydreamed of what it would be like to leave the circle and sit on some other beach towel, with other kids who could hear and who had hearing parents. These thoughts, however, were followed immediately by waves of sadness and shame. I loved my parents and could not imagine having any others, hearing or deaf.

Besides, outside the circle I could easily get lost.

To be lost in Coney Island on a Sunday in August was a scary experience, especially if your parents were deaf. While lost, eventually you'd be approached by a sympathetic adult who would take you to the nearest lifeguard station. There, the lifeguard would ask your name, and armed with that information, he would dangle you over the railing of his elevated perch, blowing his whistle in a series of earsplitting screeches. In our case, of course, the whistle was useless. The sound fell on what were literally deaf ears. We could only hope that our parents would eventually notice we were missing, and maybe, just maybe, stop talking to their friends long enough to come looking for us.

I had seen this drama play out too many times. No matter how curious I was about leaving our circle, I knew better than to venture too far.

By late afternoon, when the last of the arrivals had finally made it, there were well over one hundred beach chairs in a perfect circle. A deaf man or woman occupied each chair. And each man or woman was signing frantically to another man or woman in the circle, sometimes to one clear across the circle, far away. There were few secrets in the deaf community at Coney Island.

Suddenly I noticed someone was signing at me. It was my father. "What do the waves sound like?" his hands asked me, out of the blue. "I see them crashing onto the shore. They must make sound."

I was building a sandcastle. I had water-dampened and hardened sand walls. Three tall mud-dripped turrets stood atop a fantastical-looking structure, adorned with battlements and scooped window openings. A bridge crossed a moat. And I was now building small soldiers to stand guard. I pretended I didn't see my father's hands.

He shook me, not too gently. "What do the waves sound like?" he repeated.

It was no use. *Here we go again*, I thought. "Loud," I answered him without thinking. "Loud they must be," he signed patiently, "but many things are loud. I feel loudness through the soles of my feet. But every loud thing must be loud in its own way."

He had me there.

"Well…" I sighed while signing, trying to show that I was not sure of my answer but would do the best I could. "They sound wet when they crash down on the sand."

As soon as I said that, I knew my father would ask what wet sounded like. No sooner had my fingers touched my lips and then opened and closed against my thumbs as they made the sign for *wet* than my father demanded, "What kind of wet? Wet like a wild river? Wet like soft rain? Wet like sad tears?"

I was stumped, and more than ever, I wanted to leave the circle and find a different part of the beach to build my sandcastle.

"Wet like waves!" I finally signed. "Waves sound like a billion wet drops breaking apart when they smack down on the hard sand, all the tiny sounds joining to make one great sound. A wet, falling ocean sound," I added desperately.

My father took me into his arms and held me. Letting go, he got down on his knees in the sand and signed, "That's better. I understand now."

CHAPTER 13

The Smell of Reading

In addition to our weekly trips to the beach, another weekend destination for my family was the local Chinese restaurant. Once a month on a Saturday afternoon, as regular as clockwork, my father, with great ceremony, took my mother, my brother, and me out for lunch. Eating out was a very big deal for our family. The country was still stuck in the Depression, and the economic benefits of America's fighting a world war had not yet trickled down to our corner of the world.

On one of these monthly excursions, when I was ten

years old, we all dressed for the occasion, I in my newest R. H. Macy's suit, my brother in the latest fashion for small kids, my mother in her best dress, topped with her fox-fur stole—yes, the same fox my father had killed in their closet so many years before—and my father in his tweed suit.

Once my father had examined my brother and me for stray hairs, unnoticed stains, and scuffed shoe leather, we took the elevator to the ground floor. After a final careful look at each one of us, my father pushed open the heavy lobby door, and we exited, linked together in a line, heading toward Kings Highway. We walked up our block, eyes straight ahead. As usual, our neighbors watched us every step of the way, and after we had passed, I heard the unfailingly unchanged comments: "Considering they're deaf mutes, they dress well." "See how nice the dummies dress their boys." "The father's a deaf mute, but he has a good job."

As for the neighbors' use of the term *dummies*, I had heard it from an early age. For that matter, I'd heard my neighbors use plenty of bad words, most of which were put-downs for people from a particular place or another. But somehow *dummies* always felt especially cruel.

When my neighbors said it, they weren't speaking generally about a group of people. They were talking about the only deaf people they knew: my father and mother. Nonetheless, I was numb to their attacks, and I definitely was not going to let them ruin our monthly outing.

The Chinese restaurant was located on the ground floor of a row of two-story wooden buildings. The street-level spaces were all filled with shops: bakery, poultry, shoe repair, hardware, vegetable, pharmacy, barber, beauty, and, of course, the neighborhood candy store—home of ruby-red wax lips.

Once we were inside and seated, the highlight of the trip began: the sight of my father conversing with our Chinese waiter. To start, my father pointed at a stained plastic-covered menu, filled with columns of incomprehensible Chinese characters alongside garbled, equally incomprehensible English translations. Then, in an attempt to make his order clear, he began to sign in broken gestures he hoped our waiter would understand.

The waiter, meanwhile, politely screamed the evening's specialty at my father, as if by sheer volume my father would hear the description of the delicacy.

In response, my father would just as loudly scream his gestures of approval right back at the waiter. Neither understood the other. No meaningful information passed between them. But neither one would admit it. Instead, they kept their heads nodding in perfect smiling agreement throughout the astonishing performance.

As for me, what would otherwise have been yet another embarrassing situation was turned funny. The other diners were regulars and were used to this scene, and I could tell they were staring at our table in amusement rather than disgust. I would settle for that.

On this particular Saturday, we had our usual Chinese lunch, beginning with the specialty of the house (always the same, month after month)—an inedible, bone-filled soggy whitefish with a pair of bulging, sightless eyes, which stared at me in silent accusation. This was followed by two choices from column A (always the same choices, month after month), and one from column B (ditto), washed down with a thinly colored green liquid filled with floating black flecks. The meal ended, as it always did, with a fortune cookie, which was much prized and heartily laughed over by my parents but made absolutely no sense to me, although I liked the taste of the cookie.

But on this day, there was a change in the ritual.

After a close study of the bill, which other than the total cost was an indecipherable list of chicken scratch, my father paid for our meal. Then he turned to me and signed, "You can read now. It's time for you to get a library card."

I knew that the local library was housed in the same building as the Chinese restaurant, but I had never stepped inside. The older kids said the place contained every book that had ever been printed in the whole world. I wanted to believe them. But because you needed a library card to enter, I had no idea if that was actually true.

Every book? Why, there must be hundreds of them, I thought. But then, the older kids could not be trusted. Most everything they told us turned out to be greatly overblown. Still, since I had just learned to read well, I was curious: every book?

My father and mother were great readers. Because they were deaf, their sole source of daily entertainment was books. Our little apartment was filled with

THE SMELL OF READING

books—books of all kinds. Some books contained pictures of far-off places, showing pyramids, camels, and endless sand. Others featured giant rivers, high waterfalls, deep canyons, strange beasts, and sailing ships.

I especially loved the pictures of wooden-hulled, canvas-masted, cannon-armed sailing vessels that were shown breaking through giant, frothy waves. And ever since I had learned to read the words under these pictures, I had dreamed of having a library card of my own—a dream that was now apparently about to be realized.

Exiting the door of the Chinese restaurant, we made a hard right and entered the next door over, leading to a steep flight of wooden stairs. At the top was a painted glass door proclaiming *Brooklyn Public Library*. Pushing it open, my father led us into a single large room. The first thing I noticed was that it was filled, end to end, top to bottom, with every book that had ever been printed in the whole world. I was sure of it. The second was that the place smelled like a Chinese restaurant. It turned out the library was directly above the restaurant kitchen.

I could hardly believe that the hundreds of books lining the shelves were free for me to check out. The

Depression had me taught that everything had a price. Everything. The idea that by simply presenting a library card—nothing more than a piece of cardboard—I would be allowed to remove these precious books seemed impossible.

At first, I found the trust placed in me almost overwhelming. I examined every single page of a book before I dreamed of checking it out. If there was even a single crease at the corner of a page—or (the horror!) a food stain—I would bring that blemish to the attention of the librarian. And she would note on the flyleaf in her spidery handwriting, "Peanut butter stain? p. 36." Or, all too commonly, "Underlining. p. 12."

What I found most miraculous about the library was the sheer quantity of words to be found in the seemingly endless army of books marching shoulder to shoulder, row upon row on the shelves. Words. Words. Words. Written words. Preserved words. The library was a warehouse of words. Words to decipher. Words to learn. Words to add to my vocabulary. Words to make mine.

The words found in books were much different from my first language, the language of sign. Sign is made up

of hand shapes, hand positionings, facial expressions, and body movements. In sign, a picture really is worth a thousand words. And a sign's meaning is taken in all at once, through the eyes.

Written language, on the other hand, needs the brain for interpretation. Markings on the page must be translated into letters, and letters need to be grouped into words, and words built into sentences. Meaning forms slowly, in the brain.

When I was younger, written English seemed strange to me, and I would often go back to using sign in my head. But the more I read, the more I started to appreciate printed words. I found myself staring at each word, sounding it out in my mind for the sheer pleasure it gave me. Every word was like a musical note. It could be enjoyed on its own as well as for the sound it made when combined with other words. Best of all was the melody I heard in a perfect sentence.

Our local branch of the Brooklyn Library became my refuge. It was better, way better, than my roof for this purpose. Armed with a library card, I escaped to this quiet sanctuary anytime I became overwhelmed by the demands that my father placed on me. Here in this musty, sweet-smelling place filled with the faint odor of soy sauce, I could open a book and be magically transported to the ends of the earth.

And so I came to spend more and more time in that library, surrounded by all the words I could ever hope to learn, listening to the music of those words in my mind, while immersed in the comforting scent of Chinese food.

CHAPTER 14

Tarzan in the Jungle

While my regular trips to the beach and to the library provided an escape from the cramped, busy streets of my neighborhood, I often longed to visit less familiar confines. And like every other kid in Brooklyn in 1943, I was a huge fan of the King of the Jungle, Tarzan. I saw every one of his movies at our local theater, the Avalon, the week it was released. And I bought every one of his comic books the minute it hit the rack at the candy store.

Watching Tarzan's extraordinary ability to climb trees like an ape and to swing between trees on vines that grew in the trees' upper reaches inspired me to try my own vine-swinging feats. So I swiped a length of clothesline and fashioned a Brooklyn version of a jungle vine.

One day, with my "vine" wound tightly around my waist, I climbed a tree that stood in the backyard of our apartment building. All day long, I scampered up and down the length of the tree, my clothesline vine attached to one of its topmost branches so that I could swing in soaring arcs that took me over our neighbor's garage roof. Eventually, having used up the possibilities of creating an African jungle experience in one tree, I lay down along a limb and thought up other adventures.

I'd had plenty of success climbing a tree trunk and swinging from the end of the clothesline, so I figured that like Tarzan, I wouldn't have a problem using this as a way to travel all around my "jungle"—West Ninth Street, Brooklyn, New York.

But in my jungle, the trees were few and far between. Swinging from one to another would have required skills that I didn't think even Cheetah, Tarzan's chimp side-kick, had mastered. But I was determined to push my skills to the limit, so I settled for the next best thing: the telephone cables that snaked their way, high overhead, from pole to pole, through the backyards of my street. Looking up at them, I imagined a thick jungle canopy to swing through on my clothesline vine.

One afternoon, vine wound tightly around my waist, I climbed a telephone pole in my backyard. Grasping the cable at the top, I began my progress above the backyards of my block, making my way slowly, hand over hand, from one pole to the next, until I reached Avenue P at the end of my street. Not bad, I thought, and turning around on the cable, I made my way in the opposite direction until I reached Quentin Road. If Tarzan had lived in Brooklyn, I wondered, could he have done any better?

If any neighbors had happened to look out their back windows, they would have seen a kid with a clothes-line wound in coils around his waist, dangling from the telephone wires, with a determined look of absolute concentration on his face. *Yes*, I *was* the King of My Jungle, I thought.

Luckily for me, no one did see me—well, at least no one reported me to my parents, and I figured anyone in their right mind certainly would have if they had. As a result, I was able to perform this feat several days in a row. But I soon got tired of the single pathway running up and down the "rooftop" of my jungle, and I returned to my collection of Tarzan comics to try to find new possibilities.

Using the amazing powers of deduction that all Brooklyn kids were genetically given to enable them to transform their mundane environment into something more exciting, I came up with the idea that the brick face of my apartment building was the face of a jungle cliff. When I looked up at the wall, all I could imagine was Tarzan climbing a sheer cliff, with a hungry lion nipping at his heels. Holding that image in my mind, I imagined a lion on West Ninth Street stealthily stalking *me*.

And so it was that one day I found myself clinging to the face of my apartment building wall, like a giant, awkward spider, fingers and sneaker toes jammed between the bricks, two stories above the ground. It was slow going, but inch by inch I proceeded upward, the hot breath of the lion warming my feet, and his deep, coughing voice echoing in my ear.

Ignoring the screams of the neighborhood mothers rising from the street below me, I crawled up and up, mindful of the fire-escape railings just inches to my right. My plan was to grab the rail if I began to fall.

Just at that moment, Mrs. Abromovitz emerged backward from her bedroom window, rags in hand, to perform her once-a-week window-cleaning ritual. Settling herself comfortably on the windowsill, she lowered the overhead window onto her lap for security, turned, and saw me clinging to the wall, inches from her face. Her single scream put to shame the collective yells from the crowd on the street who had noticed the scene. Their voices were like a murmuring breeze, split by the thunder of her voice. I was so startled, I barely kept hold of the wall.

The lowered window kept Mrs. Abromovitz nailed to the windowsill, as she sat stunned in fright. I froze, stuck to the face of the building, paralyzed by the sound. Regaining my wits, I knew I had to get out of there quickly. But up or down? Down below waited my imaginary foul-breathed lion *and* the outraged neighbors, who were even more fearsome predators, so up I went, up to our apartment's third-floor fire escape.

As my mother was deaf, she did not hear me climb through her bedroom window. And since I had my own key to our apartment, she did not know that I had entered it from the fire escape. Not for the first time, I realized that for a kid like me, there were some advantages to having deaf parents.

But there was a reckoning.

That evening, when my father came home from work, three of our neighbors were stationed at our front door. They had each written down their version of my escapade, and now they jabbed the resulting stories in my father's tired face.

Mrs. Abromovitz had yet to emerge from her apartment. Apparently, the shock from seeing me outside her window had sent her straight to bed, where her husband was now faithfully caring for her.

My father and I had an interesting conversation that night, a conversation that challenged my signing comprehension to the maximum. But, as ever, my father's expressive use of his beloved language left no doubt in my mind of what lay in store for me should I *ever again* attempt a similar stunt.

The lion was not seen or heard from again on our block. The fearsome sounds of my neighbors had no doubt driven him back to Africa.

CHAPTER 15

What's in a Name

On my street, Paul Abruzzi's nickname was Paulie; Frank was known as Frankie; Thomas, Tommy; John, Johnny; Ronald, Ronnie; and my pal Harold was called Heshie. I was the one kid on my block whose name, Myron, could not easily be turned into a nickname. But that didn't stop my friends from giving me one: Mike—and then, of course, Mikey.

Although I liked spending time by myself, where I didn't need to constantly explain my deaf family to my hearing friends, there were times when I got lonely and wanted to hang out with other kids my age. And during those times, it was a pleasant change for me to hear them use my nickname, like I was one of the gang.

But I could not tell my parents about my nickname. My mother would have been horrified, not to mention offended, if she had known that I had abandoned what was to her the beautiful-sounding name she had selected for me.

But as beautiful as my mother thought my name sounded (even though she could not hear it spoken out loud), it was tedious and time-consuming for her to finger spell every letter of my name whenever she wanted to address me. It would be like a hearing person needing to stop and say each letter of someone's name before continuing with a sentence. So my mother set out to come up with another name, a nickname for me that could be signed quickly and conveniently. Nicknames such as this are called name-signs.

A name-sign is not decided on lightly. After all, it is the way the parent will address the child for the rest of his childhood—and often for the rest of his life.

My mother loved the name Myron so much that she wanted it to be recalled in my name-sign, which was why her first attempt at creating one for me involved using the initials of my name, *M* and *U*. My mother reasoned that *MU* must sound like the noise that cows make—"MOO." Looking at me one day, she shaped her hands into what looked like a cow's horns, curling the three middle fingers inward to the palm, and extending the thumb and pinkie. These horns she placed on the side of her head, thumbs touching her temples, and twisted them forward while sounding out in her voice, "MOOOO." "*M-Y-R-O-N*," she finger spelled. "How do you like this name?"

I didn't!

The ideal name-sign contains in one visual gesture the very essence of the child. With this in mind, my mother's second idea for a name-sign for me must have seemed like a no-brainer. One morning, as I was about to run downstairs to play, she stopped me in my tracks.

"Wait! I have a new name for you," she signed. She was sure that this time she had come up with something that truly captured the nature of her beloved child—the boy who seemed more comfortable high up on the limb of a tree or climbing walls. She looked into my eyes and began to scratch her sides repeatedly—which, of course, is the sign for *monkey*.

Needless to say, I also rejected this name-sign. I imagined my mother coming up to me in the street while I was playing with my friends and addressing me with the sign for *monkey*. It would have been embarrassing for both of us! Anything that singled me out from the crowd or marked me as different was something I wanted to avoid at all costs. I wanted to be Mikey, not Monkey.

Unable to find a name-sign that I would accept, my mother went back to the way she had addressed me since she named me as a baby—"MHHHAAARINNN."

CHAPTER 16

Brooklyn Bully

Freddy was the bully of our block, the curse of my existence. He was the angriest kid in our neighborhood. Maybe the angriest kid in all of Brooklyn. He was mad from sunup to sundown, and every kid in the neighborhood was his natural enemy. I sometimes wondered about this. What was Freddy so angry about? What did we ever do to him? Not to mention, why had Freddy singled me out for his special attention? He always seemed to be waiting for me to cross his path.

As he chased me, just a few strides behind, I often

wished I were four inches taller and thirty pounds heavier. But I wasn't, and with that knowledge, I increased my speed a notch—I had more than one notch—leaving him gasping, behind. Safe again.

I could outrun Freddy, but I couldn't always outthink him. As I was the only kid on our block he was unable to run down, I held a special place in his heart. His daily goal was to catch me off guard and administer his infamous arm burn.

When Freddy caught a kid, always smaller than he was, he would grab the boy's arm in his ham-hock hands, and then twist, each fat hand going in the opposite direction from the other. The result was always the same: a mighty howl of pain from the unfortunate boy, and a forearm as red as if it had been placed over a Bunsen burner.

If the burn failed to motivate the boy to ask for peace, Freddy administered his knuckle rap: a short, sharp *pang* on the head with his pointed knuckle, which was, unlike his hand, fat free and quite pointy. For the unlucky boy with a crew cut, this procedure raised a knot on his head the size of an egg. Such was the outcome of Freddy catching you.

The fact that I was fast enough to outrun him and quick enough to squirm away when he cornered me in an alley drove him crazy. Especially when, just out of his reach, I would laugh and taunt him. This proved to be my undoing.

Freddy was not stupid. A bit clumsy maybe, slow-footed for sure, but not slow-witted. Freddy came up with a plan—a plan to silence my insults and my humiliating escapes, potentially forever.

The roof of my apartment building was my private park, the one place on our busy Brooklyn block where I could go and be completely by myself. I'd gotten a copy of the primitive key that secured the heavy metal door. It was my most precious possession. With it, I could leave the noise and activity of my block. I could sit and read a book, or wonder about my life, or just look at the clouds sailing by in the blue sky.

Sometimes I even allowed myself to imagine my parents could hear, and that they had been hiding this fact from me all these years. But that was wishful thinking on my part. For if that were true, in an instant they could reveal their ability to hear, and we would magically be transformed into an ordinary family. The instant pleasure this idea produced—that my life could change completely if only my parents stopped pretending—made me feel guilty, and I quickly erased the thought from my mind. They were deaf. I could hear, and that was that.

On a clear day, I could catch glimpses of the ocean reflecting the early-morning light just beyond Coney Island, three miles away. Needless to say, I sometimes let my guard down when I was on the roof, and one fateful afternoon, it almost led to my undoing.

Without me knowing it, Freddy had studied my movements over the course of a week. Making careful note of my sudden disappearances, he followed silently behind as I took myself to the roof one day.

Usually I used my secret key to lock the metal roof door behind me as soon as I got there. But this particular afternoon, in my rush to read a new book, I forgot. Deeply engrossed in the predicament of the main character, I failed to hear Freddy creeping up on me. And when I finally heard his feet sliding across the graveled roof, it was almost too late.

Leaping to my feet, I threw my book at his head and ran by him as he ducked out of the way. I was lucky that it was a thick book. It contained many chapters, many adventures. If I'd been reading a comic book, my fate would have been sealed then and there.

But my sense of relief was brief. I dashed to the door, only to find that Freddy had jammed it shut. Left with no other choice, I ran. Like a rat in a maze, I weaved my way around the sheets hanging from the clotheslines and around the chimney stacks and air vents jutting up from the roof, Freddy hot on my heels.

Slowly but surely, Freddy herded me into a corner. I was trapped.

The next thing I knew, I was dangling, head down, over the edge of the roof, Freddy's meaty hands holding my ankles.

Strangely, I was not afraid. Instead, I was fascinated to see the ground six floors below my head. I had a bird's-eye view of the clotheslines that reached out from each apartment window. If Freddy let me go, I thought, I would bounce off the clotheslines, like a steel ball bouncing off the bumpers of a pinball machine before ending its journey—in the slot at the bottom of the machine—without a scratch.

I couldn't help wondering where I would end up if dropped. But since I was not a steel ball and was unlikely to end without a scratch, I dismissed *that* question from my mind.

Then a new image came into my mind: on the way down, I might get trapped in one of Mrs. Abromovitz's pairs of ballpark-size bloomers, hanging from her clothesline.

It's remarkable how your imminent death focuses your mind. I could see in perfect detail the shocked look on Mrs. Abromovitz's face as she reeled me in along with the rest of her laundry. The image of her surprised face was so hilarious that I burst into laughter.

This was the thing that saved me. Hearing me laugh, Freddy apparently thought he had failed to scare the wits out of me, and having never actually intended to drop me (I hoped), he pulled me back onto the roof.

From then on, Freddy never bothered me again. He had done his worst, and I had laughed in his face. He had never encountered such bravery before. I had passed some insane test that only he could decipher. And I became the envy of every other kid on the block.

CHAPTER 17

The New Girl

Unlike on my street, where everyone knew my family, at my school, which was just four blocks away, my parents' deafness was completely unknown. It was my secret, and because of this, I could be anonymous, undistinguished from all the other kids. As far as my classmates and my teachers were concerned, I was just another kid who kept to himself. I had no friends in my class, and that was exactly how I liked it. No friends, no questions.

Then one day everything changed.

On the first day of a new school year, I spotted a new member of our class. Our desks were arranged alphabetically, and because I was a *U*, I sat in the back of the room, while she, a *W*, sat in a desk to my right, immediately under a window. And the first day I saw her, the sunlight seemed to form a golden ring around her head. She looked like an angel. A small, straight nose with freckles and an ever-smiling mouth filled with unbelievably white teeth completed the picture. Her name was Eve.

The second thing I noticed about Eve was her left hand. Actually, what I noticed was the absence of her left hand. She kept it in her lap the entire hour. And when she stood to read, she pushed it deep into the pocket of her dress. This seemed odd to me, and awkward. It meant that she had to hold the heavy book of poems she was reciting from with one hand.

A week of classes passed before the mystery was solved. One morning, she sneezed. She was dipping her pen in the inkwell of her desk with her right hand when the sneeze overcame her, so when she sneezed, she brought her left hand to her mouth. It was then I saw that her left pinkie curled over the finger next to it. The pinkie looked like the crook of a shepherd's staff.

Eve saw me staring at her hand and quickly dropped it into her lap, where it lay hidden beneath her desktop. Staring straight ahead, with a fixed expression on her face, she blushed. I could tell I had embarrassed her.

As the school year went on, I noticed that my classmates also became aware of Eve's hand. They would stare whenever it made a rare appearance. Some would even laugh. Eve would cringe at their stares and shrink at the sound of their laughter.

She never stood straight. She was taller than the rest of the class, and she tried to blend into the crowd by slumping. But when our classmates laughed, she didn't just slump, she practically hunched over. Often, the laughter was not even directed at her. Our classmates laughed at just about anything. But for Eve, every laugh was about her and her misshapen hand.

Whenever I saw that Eve was uncomfortable, I felt uncomfortable too. I knew what it was like to feel different. Well, in my case, it was my parents who were different, but the shame I felt because of them was the same shame that Eve seemed to feel about her hand. I knew what it was like to want to shrink into the crowd, to become anonymous. I decided we should be friends.

It took some time, but after a while Eve became comfortable around me. Though she lived just around the corner on West Tenth Street, *around the corner* was another world altogether. My friends and I on West Ninth had no need to ever leave our block. There was absolutely nothing on West Tenth Street that was not available to me right outside our apartment building door—until I met Eve. Soon I was carrying Eve's books home at the end of every school day. And I arranged to meet her at the stoop in front of her two-family house every morning before school.

Eventually, Eve introduced me to her mother. I figured out she didn't have a father, but I thought it was best not to ask what had happened. After some time had passed, I asked Eve to come to my house. She agreed, and when the time came, I introduced her to my mother. I hadn't told Eve in advance that my mother was deaf. I didn't know how to. And somehow, I knew that it wouldn't matter to Eve.

As I signed to my mother to introduce my new friend, I could see the surprise flash across Eve's face, but she didn't stare or act different in any way. After the introductions were done, she asked me all sorts of questions. How did I learn sign language? How did I communicate with my parents before I learned? Had they always been deaf? Why wasn't I deaf as well? Her questions weren't embarrassing, because it seemed as though she was genuinely interested in my answers.

I had some questions of my own for her. Were you born that way? Did you get your hand caught in a door? Can a doctor straighten out your pinkie? I don't think my questions embarrassed her either.

In time, she asked me to teach her some signs. As most signs require two hands to execute, she had some difficulty at first. But eventually she lost her self-consciousness in front of me and learned even the most complex signs I could teach her. Using both hands, she showed off her signing to my mother, who signed back, "Very clear. Very beautiful signs." And I translated my mother's approval to Eve.

One day, our teacher told the class that every morning

of the following month we would begin the day with a student doing a demonstration of some kind of learning project. The project was ours to choose. Our teacher suggested some possibilities for our consideration. We could prepare a science project, for instance, involving butterflies in a jar. As she said this, every kid had the identical thought: butterflies in Brooklyn? Groans of protest spread throughout the classroom.

"Or possibly you could show us worms burrowing into their habitat," she suggested. Where would we find worms? Practically all of Brooklyn was paved over. More groans. "Or you could make an ant farm." Finally, we thought, here at last is a practical suggestion. We all knew where to find ants on our block. But we couldn't all present ant farms.

Having exhausted her supply of ideas, our teacher gave up. "*Any* project will be satisfactory." She added, "Originality and mastery of the project are what counts. Make it interesting. And if you wish, you may pair up and present the project jointly."

I looked at Eve, and Eve looked at me. In unspoken agreement, we decided we would join forces to prepare and present a project. But what could we do? After much discussion in the lunchroom, we came up with an idea. An excellent idea, we thought. It would be original, as the teacher insisted. It would be interesting. We were sure of that. Now all we had to do was to master it. Or, at least, Eve would have to, since we had decided to do a sign language project. We would call it "Writing on Air."

For the next four weeks, Eve and I spent most of our spare time after school practicing signing on her front stoop. We were so energetic that we drew a crowd of fascinated neighborhood kids.

"Teach us. Teach us," they clamored. "We want to learn your secret language."

This was a new phenomenon for me.

Usually, in public I signed as quickly and with as few signs as possible when responding to my parents' questions. My answers tended to be abrupt, shorthand versions of what are usually elaborate, expressive signs. I had always been embarrassed to sign in public. But now something had changed, and I reveled in the attention my knowledge of this exotic form of communication was getting. I began to show off with exaggerated gestures some of the more complicated signs my father had taught me. The signs were basically a vocabulary list, and they made no sense together, but that didn't matter. What mattered was the complexity and dexterity of the sign itself.

My sign for *acrobat* brought down the house. My father had recently taken me to the Ringling Brothers Circus at Madison Square Garden and had taught me many circus signs. These were all new to me. There had never been a need for them in our apartment. But once I'd learned them, I found any excuse to use them. "Look, Mom," I signed, as I jumped onto my bed. "I'm an *acrobat.*"

My right index and middle fingers, shaped like the legs of an acrobat, stood on my open left upturned palm. Then the "legs" on my right hand flexed, jumped, flipped over, and executed a double somersault, before descending back onto my left palm, where they stood, triumphant, slightly quivering from the impact. My sign was so good that I could swear you could see the sawdust covering the circus arena of my left palm. At least, I could—and my mother applauded.

Of course, all the kids in the neighborhood wanted to know "secret" signs—words they could send back and forth without adults knowing what they were saying. By far the best of these signs was the one for *poop*. To make this sign, the right thumb is grasped in the fist of the left hand. Then slowly (or quickly, if the person has been eating prunes) the thumb is drawn down from the enclosed right fist. The onlookers loved it. Now every kid in the neighborhood could say *poop* in sign.

Finally, the day arrived to present our projects in front of the class. Numbly, I sat through the most boring displays and incomprehensible explanations of why fireflies light up (which they absolutely refused to do in their jelly-jar home, being otherwise occupied sucking on the grape jelly under the lid). When this less-than-thrilling description petered out, we were treated to an elaborate description of where a mosquito goes to die after biting you. This display featured ten dead mosquitoes lying peacefully on a bed of leaves at the bottom of an airless jar that a kid had neglected to puncture with a nail. Then a classmate informed us, in way too much detail, how a moth turns into a butterfly. This one the class didn't believe for a minute. Finally, it was our turn.

Eve and I had planned to stand at the front of the class.

She would stand behind me, where I couldn't see her, and she would hold up—in her right hand, of course—a drawing of the sign I was supposed to perform. When she called out the word for the sign, I would execute it from memory in a kind of visual spelling bee.

When we were introduced by the teacher, half the class decided it was the perfect time to try out the "secret" sign Eve and I had taught them. All together, they made the sign for *poop*. The other half of the class nearly fell out of their chairs laughing. The teacher stood, dumbstruck, not having a clue what was going on. The room was a bedlam of hands in motion. *Poop*, *Poop*, *Poop* signs flew through the air—were *flung* through the air. It was a hailstorm of *poops*. A tornado of *poops*.

It took at least fifteen minutes for the teacher to restore order.

Once again, she introduced Eve and me, with the warning that any further outburst, whatever it was about, would be rewarded with a trip to the principal's office.

We began. Eve called out *penguin*, and I dropped both my hands, palms facing downward, fingers held together, to either side of my waist. Then, hunching up my shoulders, I raised and lowered each one, one at a time. To emphasize this sign, I lurched forward, stiff-legged, mimicking the lumbering walk of a penguin as it traversed an ice floe. The class clapped.

Eve asked for *deer*. Now I made what I imagined was the face of a startled deer, possibly caught in the headlights of a car on Flatbush Avenue, placing both my open hands above my head, all ten fingers spread and shooting out into stiff antler appendages. These I wiggled convincingly as the class broke into a cheer.

"Elk?"

I was an elk.

"Moose?"

I was a moose.

The class loved it. "More. More!"

"Elephant?" My right hand formed a cup with its back resting against my nose. My hand moved slowly and gracefully out from my nose, curving downward, while my hand turned under, looking for peanuts that were now visible to the imagination on the dirt floor of the circus ring of our minds.

The class erupted. My signs were killing them. This

had to be better than ten dead mosquitoes and a bunch of fireflies that would not light. Eve took me through a jungle of animals and a zoo full of exotic birds.

Then she began a list of more complex signs that we had agreed upon. The first sign was for a concept we were both familiar with. "What is the sign for embarrass?" she asked.

I made the sign for *red*, as in *blood*, moving my index finger up and down my red lips. Then both of my palms cradled my face, moving slowly upward, as if the red blush of blood was rising, filling my entire face in blossoming mortification. The class was fascinated.

Then Eve asked, "What is the sign for *discard*?" and I drew a blank. I stood mute.

Eve prompted again, "Discard?"

I stood there at the front of the class, all eyes focused on me, my hands at my sides, defeated. Now a genuine blush of embarrassment was flooding my face. Somehow, I had completely forgotten this sign.

Eve realized that there was no use in asking me again.

She dropped the cards and rushed to my side to rescue me. *Discard* is a sign that requires both hands to execute.

Without a moment's hesitation, she removed her left hand from her pocket and lifted it into the air, palm open and facing the class, pinkie finger crooked in its permanently twisted position. Then with her open right hand, she drew her fingertips across the palm of her left hand toward her pinkie.

Suddenly, she closed her right hand, as if clasping something, and swiftly withdrew it from her left palm, where she had discovered the imaginary object. Then with a forceful motion, she flung the object to the floor, all the while making an expression of such disgust that the class fully expected the terrible object to leap up and scurry out of the room.

The audience was stunned into silence by Eve's performance. Everyone understood what Eve had done, what her sign had signified.

No one laughed.

Suddenly, the class erupted into shouts of approval. Now Eve blushed not in embarrassment but from pride.

From that day on, she never hid her hand again.

CHAPTER 18

The Palmer Method

I always felt that sign was my main language, and that written English, while necessary, was not as good for communicating the things I was thinking and feeling. Unfortunately, my teachers did not share this belief, and sign was not a regular part of my schoolwork. Penmanship, on the other hand, was.

One day in third grade, I came home from school with a notebook filled with lines of gorgeous letters, all in a row, bounding across the page like a herd of prancing gazelles. These, sadly, were not created by me. Mine were the ones sandwiched between these soaring lines of grace, and they looked more like lines of fat, crawling caterpillars.

This had been my first exposure to the dreaded Palmer method of penmanship, which the school authorities of Brooklyn, in their wisdom, had determined was essential to the education of every budding street scholar.

The so-called method, named after the guy who dreamed it up, was actually a writing style where the letters of the alphabet are joined together in a graceful, flowing manner. To me, it was picture perfect, as if created by a writing machine, but it was boringly repetitive.

The goal was to make the writing of every kid in America indistinguishable from every other kid's writing. This meant that my writing would be the same as a girl's in North Dakota, wherever that was. What was the fun of having all of our writing be the same? I wondered. What about our own personalities?

It seemed to me that something was being lost. But remarkably, I thought, no one was interested in what I thought on this subject.

Instead, they were focused on my subpar attempts. "Myron, what on earth are these words?" my teacher had said earlier that day. "This page looks like the yard of a chicken run. What could these chicken tracks possibly mean?" I tried to explain, but in truth, some of the words were unreadable even to me. This was impressive. I had written them only a moment before.

As I listened to my traitorous classmates laughing, I watched in awe as my teacher proceeded to fill my notebook with alternating lines of graceful, elegant, mirror image letters—in alternating capitals and lowercase.

"Now, Myron, take your notebook home, and practice!"

That evening, after my mother had cleared the supper dishes from the kitchen table, I practiced my penmanship. My father sat across from me, reading his paper. In the blank lines between my teacher's beautiful gazelle-like words, I scrawled my ugly, clumsy counterparts. As I looked at my graceless efforts of duplicating my teacher's graceful examples, I realized that this was similar to my signing ability. It had always been serviceable, but by no means as beautiful as my father's elegant, flowing signs.

Putting down his paper, my father turned my notebook to him.

"What in heaven's name are you doing?" he signed.

The look on his face, accompanying his signs, was one of pure puzzlement.

"I'm practicing my penmanship."

"Is that what it is?" my father asked. "So why can't I read it?"

Not meaning to be rude, but realizing this conversation was not leading anywhere I wanted to go, I resumed my tortured, pathetic squiggles across the page.

Line after line of miserable...what? Yes, I realized, they were exactly as my teacher had said: *chicken tracks*.

I laid down my pen in utter frustration. I was beaten. And besides, my hand hurt.

Looking up at my father, I saw him break into the most exaggerated signs, punctuated with carefully sculpted finger-spelled letters of the alphabet. It was as if he were cutting the letters from a block of marble, one by one, each one letter perfect.

His signs looped and soared with the ornamental elegance of a peacock, blended with the agility of a long-tailed swallow.

"That's my Palmer method," he signed, picking up his newspaper.

CHAPTER 19

Parent-Teacher Night

Shortly after I turned nine, I was faced with my ultimate challenge as translator between my father and the outside world: the dreaded parent-teacher night. When it was announced, I knew I was doomed. My real school life—more than just my poor penmanship—was about to be exposed to my parents.

Because they were deaf, and because I was not exactly eager to tell them about my life in school, my parents had absolutely no idea of what—in their mind—their well-mannered, *genius* son was doing in school.

I was determined, at all costs, to deny them that information. I would be like the American spy captured by the Germans in the latest World War II movie I'd seen, who resisted all torture, even bamboo shoots under his fingernails. He simply would not talk. And neither would I. I would succeed, I was sure, since my parents could not hear what my teacher had to say to them.

But when I first learned that our parents were invited—and attendance was definitely not optional—to a conference with our teachers about our progress (or lack of it in my case) in our schoolwork and our social development, the news chilled me to the bone. I realized that my father would ask that I come with them to the event. For something this important, I knew he would not be satisfied with shuffling handwritten notes back and forth to my teacher. He would want me to act as his interpreter.

My father did not ask; he insisted that I go with them to this meeting. And I immediately realized what this meant. Not only would I be expected to translate, but I would be expected to pass sensitive information about myself back and forth between my father and my teacher, and the whole time I would be invisible to both.

Up until now, the world I lived in with my mother and father was my Brooklyn block. In this world, I was known as the hearing son of two deaf parents. No more. No less. And best of all, no big deal. When my mother called my name from our third-floor apartment window, no one turned to see where the piercing sound came from. When my father cheered me on during games of stickball and touch football in his hard, harsh voice, my friends didn't pay any attention to him. And when he signed to me and I signed back, no one stared. The rhythmic movements of our arms and hands and bodies as we signed were as natural a sight as the branches of the trees on our block, waving in the breeze from Coney Island.

But now, all that would change. In a few painfully short days, I would be with my parents in a huge auditorium filled with teachers and parents—strangers who had maybe never met a deaf person, heard a deaf voice, or even seen someone sign. What would they think?

Plus, I would have to translate my father's praise of my many skills and attributes to my teacher, each and every one of them. Then, in response, I would have to interpret my teacher's honest, critical, but oh-so-constructive opinions of my shortcomings. Also one by one.

The evening inevitably arrived on schedule.

"Myron, please tell your parents I'm very happy to finally meet them," my teacher said in her pleasantly soft voice.

I smiled and interpreted, word for word, my facial grammar expressing her happiness.

"Myron, please tell the teacher that we are as well," signed and voiced my father. His signs were exaggerated and his voice was harsh.

I cringed and interpreted word for word.

"Myron, please tell your parents that although you are a good student, you have a severe discipline problem."

"The teacher says I'm a pleasure to have in her class."

"Tell them that if you don't improve in deportment, conduct, and paying attention, I'll have to recommend that you be held back a grade."

"My teacher says that at the rate I'm learning, she may recommend me for skipping a grade," I signed creatively.

"Furthermore," my teacher said in her sweetly controlled voice, "tell your parents that you are the worst discipline problem I've ever encountered in all of my twenty-two years of teaching in Brooklyn schools. Myron, you are truly unique."

"My teacher says that she sees a bright future for me, perhaps as a surgeon or an airline pilot."

By now, my mother was beaming.

But my father, who had watched the very active and prolonged movement of my teacher's lips, and her facial expressions throughout the conversation, was scowling. What he was seeing and what I was signing did not match up.

"Baloney!" he signed to me in our home-sign for the word. "Baloney," he repeated in exasperation.

"Now, tell me exactly what the teacher is saying," he signed in his no-nonsense sign. My father could read the face of a hearing person like an Egyptologist could read the Rosetta stone, and he had unlocked the secrets of my teacher's face and gestures. The jig was up. The image of the American spy was gone from my mind. Now I was spilling the beans.

Looking at my father's grim face and angry gestures, my teacher said in the voice she reserved for me when I disobeyed her request to be quiet in class, "Myron, what have you been telling your father?"

"Well…" I began but couldn't continue.

"Myron, tell your father *exactly* what I'm saying to him now."

I cringed.

Seeing my discomfort, my teacher thankfully took pity on me.

"Myron is a good boy. He reads well, is obviously intelligent, but he has a discipline problem." Then she smiled and said, "He has ants in his pants." Reflecting on her own metaphor, she added, "And there are times I'm tempted to *squash* him, like an ant."

The sign for *ant* is iconic in sign language: the closed left hand is the body of an ant and sits above the back of the right hand, which moves forward while the fingers wiggle furiously like an ant's legs. In my newfound honesty, to get rid of any doubt in my father's mind as to *exactly* what my teacher meant by this statement, I followed with the second version of this sign: the hands are closed in fists, and the right extended thumbnail comes down repeatedly against the left thumbnail, squashing an army of ants between the thumbnails. I executed this sign with such descriptive power that my mother smiled—and nodded vigorously in agreement—while my father collapsed in laughter that was interrupted by an emphatically barked "*Yes! Yes!*" followed by his sign for, "Sometimes, same me! Squash Myron, like ant."

As my father made the exaggerated signs for "squashing Myron like ant," my teacher joined in the hilarity, all at my expense. But I didn't care. I had escaped any further elaboration of my transgressions in her class.

Soon, however, I noticed that this lively exchange had made our little group the center of attention for every parent and teacher in the room. People stared with gaping mouths and looks of astonishment on their faces.

No way, I thought. *I'll be as tough as my father.* And I proceeded to stare right back at them.

That night, after we returned to our apartment, and my father had paid the neighbor who'd watched my brother while we were out, my mother made hot cocoa and topped it off with my favorite, fresh-whipped cream, made by hand. When I finished drinking my cocoa, she let me scoop the remaining fluffy pile of whipped cream from the bowl directly into my mouth, and when my brother complained, into his mouth too. I couldn't imagine why, but she was pleased with me.

My father was another matter. He was as serious as I'd ever seen him with me. Looking at me sternly, he signed, "Myron, no more of your foolishness in school. I expect a better report from your teacher at the next parent-teacher meeting." Then, while holding my gaze, he hesitated and added, "And if you don't…" and he made the sign for squashing an ant, and burst into laughter.

CHAPTER 20

A Boy in Uniform

After learning of my performance in school, my father began to think of ways to get me to shape up. And in 1944, at the height of the US war effort in World War II, the perfect opportunity presented itself: getting involved in an organization that would teach me some military-style discipline while also showing pride in my country.

Boy Scouts.

I had grown up hearing stories about the war. Every night after dinner, while my mother was doing the evening dishes, my father sat at the kitchen table and read to us—in sign—from the first page of the *New York Daily News*, which his work in the composing room had helped to create. In the early years, the war had gone badly. The Allied nations, which the United States would later join, were losing on every front, one battle after another.

"Don't worry," my father's hands had told my brother and me. "America has never lost a war." I'd been able to read most of the words on the front page for myself. But I liked to watch my father read the front page to me. Words like *war* and *battle* and *army* and *shell* and *bomb* were just words to me. So were words like *wounded* and *death*. But when these words were turned into sign in my father's hands, they came alive.

In his hands, nightly, I saw the fall of bombs, the flight of shells, and the movement of armies. I could hear the cries of the wounded, and the stillness of death. I could see the explosions on the decks of ships at the Battle of Midway, the sailors abandoning ship as jagged holes appeared at the waterline, and the oil-stained sea clotted with survivors clinging to floating debris. My brother would sit, fascinated by the dramatic signs, too young to understand what all the excitement was about but loving every minute of it.

The evening readings with my father had become the high point of my day. And I became a great student of the war. My friends would have to wait to see the newsreel shown every Saturday afternoon at our local movie theater for an update on the war. I could watch it every night of the week as it played itself out on the human screen of my father's hands.

Then, in 1944, the tide of war started to turn in the Allies' favor. We were on the march. I thrilled to see my father's signs every night as he read me the headlines that told of the advances our soldiers were making up the boot of Italy.

In June, Rome was liberated.

In the same month, the Allies landed on the beaches of Normandy, in France. D-Day had finally arrived. Slowly but surely, our troops were working their way to Paris.

The newspaper was filled with pictures of soldiers in uniform, soldiers in foxholes, soldiers in chow lines, soldiers at the front, and even soldiers who had died. All in a uniform of one kind or another—theirs and ours.

I wanted a uniform of my own.

My mother's youngest brother, Milton, was a captain in the army, a paratrooper posted somewhere in Europe, and then in Burma. He sent me a bayonet holder and a bandolier, a wide leather belt he wore over his shoulders that held extra bullets for his rifle. I wore them around the apartment, the heavy bandolier hanging down to my knees.

Harry, another of my uncles, was a sailor on the USS *Missouri*, somewhere in the Pacific Ocean. He sent me a sailor's hat. It was spanking white and broken in nicely, with creases in all the right places, and I liked to wear it tilted over one eye. With my sailor hat on, I lurched around our apartment as I imagined my uncle did at the height of a storm on the Pacific, the waves crashing over the bow, roller upon roller.

Our apartment was small. And because my mother liked to wash and wax the kitchen floor every day— hourly, it seemed to me—she often chased me out of the apartment and into our third-floor hallway.

Soon the older kids in the building, all wearing scraps of a uniform—an odd hat here, a cracked leather belt there—joined me. We stomped up and down the marble-floored hallways, and clattered up and down the metal stairways, singing: "You're in the army now. You're not behind the plow. You'll never get rich by digging a ditch. You're in the army now."

Our voices echoed through the halls and up and down the stairwells, until every door of every apartment was flung open by angry neighbors shouting at us to *shut up!* and threatening to give chase if we didn't. The Germans were tough, I knew, but some of our neighbors were tougher. Mr. Kaplan, on the fourth floor, scared the life out of me. He had a small mustache, which I thought made him look like Hitler. I avoided the fourth floor at all costs. It was enemy territory.

We ran to the elevator and rode it down to the basement to escape. As soon as the door opened, we tumbled out and went running through the musty darkness, past the dim storage rooms and the ever-glowing mouth of the hungry furnace. Bursting out the cellar door, we escaped into the alley, once again safe to march and fight another day.

Exhausted, but exhilarated, I would retreat to our apartment, where I would let my brother wear my equipment, while I taught him to march and sing military songs. This attention I paid to my brother made my mother happy, but she still drew the line at our marching on her newly waxed kitchen floor, which was so shiny and slick you could ice-skate on it.

My longing for a uniform caught my father's attention. As the Allies took Paris in August, my father came home with a large, long box held under his arm. Placing it with great authority in my hands, he commanded me to open it. Inside was a brand-new, sharply creased Boy Scout uniform, complete with regulation belt, knee-high socks, pleated scarf, and lanyard.

"This is a uniform for you," he signed. "And your black Thom McAn shoes, with a good shine on them, will be perfect."

I did not know a single kid in all of Brooklyn who was a Boy Scout. There must have been a reason for this, I thought, holding the box in my arms.

While I stood there, my father marched into his bedroom and returned, still marching, with a silver-framed picture of himself, taken when he was a boy. The picture showed him dressed in his deaf-school military uniform, peaked cap and all. To me, he looked like one of the drummer boys in the Civil War pictures in our history books at school.

"You're just like me when I was your age," he signed, his index fingers coming together sharply, emphasizing the sign for *same*.

Taking me by the hand, he marched me into my bedroom. In front of the mirror, my father dressed me in my spanking-new, sharply creased Boy Scout uniform. *Now what?* I wondered.

As if reading my mind, my father signed, "The Boy Scouts are not big on marching. But discipline and obedience are important. And you could use a healthy dose of both. But don't worry, it's not all about that. You'll learn things too. And for every new subject you master, you'll get a merit badge. I'll help you with that."

The first scout meeting was held in the basement of our scout leader's home, on the other side of Seth Low Park. My father came along and waited outside until it ended.

I'd never been so bored in my life. All we did was repeat, over and over again, the Boy Scout oath. The next meetings were no better. If anything, they were worse because my father stopped coming, which meant every time I ventured out in my ridiculous blue uniform, the bullies in the neighborhood chased after me.

But my father remained enthusiastic. He'd consulted the merit badge section of the *Boy Scout Handbook*, and he was determined that I should earn one.

So after supper one night I found myself at the kitchen table, sorting through about a million postage stamps, which my father had bought at a postage store in the city. Staring up at me were strange-looking faces covered in various styles of facial hair—spade whiskers, waxy curled mustaches, even muttonchops—and an equally exotic assortment of strange beasts, all printed in a brilliant range of colors.

In the exact middle of the table sat a new stamp book, open to the first blank page, which seemed to dare me to fill it, so I could one day earn my very first merit badge: "Stamp Collecting: MB (Merit Badge) NO: 108."

My father delicately selected a stamp from the jumbled pile. Holding it carefully by the edge, he placed it in front of me. Then he handed me a pair of tweezers and a sticky piece of paper used to mount the stamp, which I learned was called a hinge. He instructed me to attach the stamp in a box outlined on the blank page of the stamp album. Without a second thought, I grasped the stamp with the tweezers and pressed it onto the glued hinge, and in the process, tore the whiskered face in half. My father groaned.

"Gently, softly," the fingers on my father's hands signed, gently, softly, ever-so-slowly squeezing an invisible object. I tried again.

This effort produced an interesting crease in the otherwise curled horns of an antelope, making it look as though the horns grew out of the poor animal's backside.

Not waiting for my father's comment, in desperation I grabbed another one of the pristine colored bits of paper and gently, softly placed it squarely on the hinge in the center of a box. I paused, letting the glue dry so that it would stick to the page.

Convinced that I had waited long enough, I gently, softly removed the tweezers—taking the entire perimeter of the stamp, now glued to the tweezers, along with it, and leaving the heart of the stamp glued to the hinge on the page.

Looking up, I saw my father's eyes cross and his lips squeeze in anguish. His hands lay silenced on top of his head. He had nothing to say.

I dug into that pile of stamps frantically, time and time again, with pretty much the same results. Finally, my father stilled my hands in his. "I have another idea," he signed.

The following week, he brought home an X-Acto knife set of carving tools. There were three knives housed in the bottom of a blond wooden case, and an assortment of extremely sharp-looking blades held by felt loops. The whole thing was a wonder to my eyes. It was magnificent. But what in the world was it for? I wondered.

"MB NO: 118. Wood Carving," my father signed to me, with an optimism I was sure was misguided.

That evening we sat, my father, my brother, and I, where we always sat when there was a project at hand— at the kitchen table. As usual, my mother was doing the dinner dishes, back turned to us, but with a definite smile on her face—a smile that threatened, I thought, to break into a belly laugh at any moment.

The X-Acto knife set sat in the middle of the table on a sheet of newspaper. Alongside the open case were three bars of Ivory soap.

"We'll break in these knives by carving the bars of

soap. That way we won't dull the blades, and you'll get practice in carving. But be careful," my father signed. "These blades are as sharp as a surgeon's scalpel."

Impatient as usual, I picked up one of the knives, and with the skill of a brain surgeon, I proceeded to slice a bar of soap neatly in two, along with the web of skin between my thumb and forefinger.

My brother, who had been eyeing the box of blades, left the table in a rush at the sight of the blood spurting from my hand. He was always complaining that I got new things first, never shared them, and passed them on to him only when they got old. But this time he lost interest in my latest gift almost immediately.

Once the blood stopped flowing and the cut was bandaged, we tried again.

"Gently, softly," my father signed. I was, frankly, getting tired of these signs.

But slowly, gently, softly, I learned to use the knives, and succeeded in carving out of the soft soap…a blob approximately the shape of a large dog. Depending on how you held it, it looked like it had horns instead of ears and a leg for a tail, or like the exotic jungle plant on one of the stamps I had ruined. But what the heck, it wasn't half bad. *I can do this*, I thought.

"Practice," my father signed. And I did. Every afternoon I carved an animal from a bar of soap, and every evening I displayed the soap model to my mother and father, while my brother looked on, a puzzled expression on his face.

"WONDERFUL," my mother would sign, exploding her open hands from the side of her face in admiration. I discounted this. I knew that everything I ever did was, according to my mother, nothing less than wonderful.

My brother stared skeptically at my latest effort. "But what is it?" he asked.

"I have no idea," my father answered, looking disgustedly at the now soft, shapeless pile. "But if it were brown I'd hold my nose!"

While we trying to figure out what that meant, he signed, yet again, "Practice."

Oh, how I hated that sign. But I did as he instructed, and in time, the bathroom was filled with grotesque soap animals of every imaginable description. We washed with elephants with one ear missing. My brother and

I bathed with soap mice and rats missing tails and ears. My father shaved with short-necked soap giraffes. And my mother did the dishes with soap nightmares, that no one, not even me, could explain. However, the scabs that formed on both my hands from countless nicks and cuts were easily identifiable.

After about a hundred bars of soap and a pint of blood, we abandoned the project known as MB NO: 118. Wood Carving. And about a week after that, my Boy Scout uniform was gently wrapped in tissue paper, mothballs, and cedar shavings, and put away in the bottom drawer of my dresser. What was the use of being a Boy Scout, my father and I agreed, if I couldn't even get one merit badge?

My brother was thrilled. Here was something, he realized, that would one day be passed down to him in virtually perfect condition. But by the time that day finally arrived, he had lost all interest. No one on our block was a Boy Scout, and for that matter, no one had *ever* been a Boy Scout. And my brother had no more interest than I did in being known as the First Boy Scout on West Ninth Street.

CHAPTER 21

Finding a Hobby

My father's quest for me to earn a Boy Scout merit badge was ultimately met with no more success than the Brooklyn Dodgers' annual quest for the World Series. But he was still determined that I follow in his footsteps and develop a hobby—any hobby.

My father was a great believer in heredity. Because I was his son, he thought I would not only enjoy having a hobby, but like him, I would be great at it. My father had many hobbies, and he was an expert in all of them. So began a steady accumulation of "sets" for me to hone my hobby skills.

My A. C. Gilbert Chemistry Set came in a sleek wooden case, secured by a brass catch. Inside were shelves containing an impressive array of chemicals in glass jars, many with cork stoppers, along with glass test tubes, tiny measuring spoons, litmus paper, and a spatula. There was even a small scale and an alcohol lamp.

Each jar of chemicals had a label on its side with strange, often impossible-to-pronounce names: *phenolphthalein, ammonium chloride, sodium carbonate, sodium ferrocyanide, cobalt chloride, calcium oxide, ferric ammonium sulfate.* On and on marched the jaw-dropping names across the rows of jars, neatly stacked in their wooden racks.

Accompanying this impressive collection of chemicals was a manual titled "Fun with Chemistry." The cover showed a young boy holding a lightning bolt.

My father instructed me to read the manual before I tried any experiment. Then he left me to enjoy my new hobby, signing, "Have fun. Experiment."

I was a fast reader and soon had scanned the two hundred odd experiments the manual promised were possible with careful use of the chemicals contained in the set.

The very next afternoon, with my mother's reluctant permission, I set up my "lab" in our bathroom.

Closing the bathroom door behind me, imagining myself the mad scientist I had seen in last week's movie, I proceeded to do "experiments."

I turned water into wine. Well, actually, clear water into rose-colored water.

I made writing ink that was invisible until heated over my alcohol flame.

I used up the supply of litmus paper, transforming the strips into a variety of stunning colors, after dipping them in my toxic brews.

By mixing four different chemicals in a test tube, I was even able to create smoke, which rose to our bathroom ceiling, where it hung like fog until I dispersed it with bathroom towels.

Then I was bored, until I remembered the boy holding the lightning bolt.

Putting aside the manual, I wondered what would happen if I mixed certain chemicals based on their color and the sound of their names.

Mixing no fewer than twelve chemicals together, I

placed the mixture above my alcohol lamp. Standing in the tub, I watched from behind the shower curtain as the flame licked at the bottom of the test tube. Slowly but surely, the mixture began to bubble...then boil.

Then it exploded.

The paint peeled from the ceiling of our bathroom. The sound of exploding glass was deafening. But the sound was not the problem. My mother did not hear a thing. It was the smell. The stink clung to everything—the sulfurous smell of Hades itself.

One whiff of the odor as it wafted into the living room from beneath the bathroom door and my mother was at the door, yanking it open. This, of course, sent a huge cloud of smoke drifting into the living room, enveloping every piece of furniture, seeping into the fabric of our couch, and eventually dying in the folds of the drapes.

"What in God's name," my father signed as he came through our front door that evening, "is that horrible smell?"

My mother quietly informed her husband that "his son" had been "experimenting." She couldn't help adding, "Just as you told him to."

Brooklyn
and Beyond

Brooklyn and Beyond

CHAPTER 22

Polio

Summer in Brooklyn was a golden time. Finally free from the daily routine of school, our summer days were wonderful and carefree, seamlessly blending one into another. But my twelfth summer, the summer of 1945, was different.

It was the height of the polio scare. Polio is a disease that can cause muscle weakness, paralysis, and even death. At the time, it was most common in children. But the most well-known sufferer of polio was an adult, Franklin Delano Roosevelt, who happened to be the president of the United States.

That year, it seemed every mother in Brooklyn was forcing down her children's throats a daily dose of castor oil, a concoction that was supposed to help fend off the disease. The thick, oily, fishy-smelling liquid clung to our lips, coated our tongues, and lined our throats for hours. It was impossible to get rid of the taste.

"It's good for you," my mother signed in annoyance at my daily objection. Often, she had to force my mouth open to get me to take the stuff. I hated fish, and I despised castor oil, the deadliest by-product of fish ever created by man. Unlike fish, castor oil may have lacked bones, but for me, it was pure, distilled evil. My brother, on the other hand, who was used to taking medicine every day to control his seizures, drank the stuff without complaining. He even seemed to like it.

"It hurts me more than it does you," my mother signed after our daily dosage had been given.

Then came the killer closer in any argument: "Do you want to get polio?"

Every day we heard about polio: "Don't get overheated. Do you want to get polio?" (This was usually followed by "That's what happened to President Roosevelt when he was a young man. Do you want to sit in a wheel-chair for the rest of your life like him?") "Don't go in the water right after eating. You'll get a cramp and die. And if not, you'll get polio." "Stay away from crowds. You'll get polio." "Don't get dirty. You'll get polio." "You can't go to the movies this Saturday. Some kid on the next block got polio." "Don't eat food if a fly lands on it. You'll get polio."

And then came the dreaded final words: "Do you want to end up in an iron lung?" The iron lung was the device that helped people with polio breathe. It was a huge, scary-looking metal drum, which enveloped much of a person's body, and it represented what we all feared most about polio—that we would spend our summer days stuck, motionless, lying in a hospital.

To put special emphasis on her daily list of *don'ts*, my mother used not one but two signs. There was the usual *don't* she used every day—the quick flick of her thumb from under her chin. And then there was the second *don't*, which she used so there would be no room for argument. She crossed her hands like an X, palms facing me for added emphasis. Then she would repeatedly separate and recross them, all the while looking at me with the most serious expression she could muster. My mother kept this up until she felt I had properly acknowledged her warnings. Not with a simple nod of my head, or a shake of my hinged fist in the sign for *yes*, but with an emphatic, finger-spelled, "*O-k-a-y! O-k-a-y! O-K-A-Y!*"

And if I ever, heaven forbid, had a sniffle or a stomachache, she sent me to bed immediately. Then, until the sniffle dried up, or the stomachache stopped aching, my mother hovered over me like a soft, enveloping cloud.

My brother was even more closely monitored. Whenever there was a reported outbreak of polio in Brooklyn, even if it was miles away, my mother would keep Irwin indoors so there wasn't even the slightest chance of him being exposed to the disease—or any other germ for that matter.

No one knew how a person got polio. Our doctor didn't. The scientists didn't. Our teachers didn't. Our parents didn't. Even Mrs. Birnbaum, who spent all day spying on our block while leaning out her window, her arms resting on a pillow, didn't. And she knew *everything*.

But my parents seemed convinced that heat was a great incubator of the polio germ, and they viewed the long days of summer with particular alarm. Every time a heat wave descended on Brooklyn, all the kids in the neighborhood were sent to their rooms.

As I played with my brother in our bedroom one day, I wondered: if an epileptic person caught polio, would his seizures stop? I also wondered if maybe deaf people could not get the disease. I had never heard of a deaf person who had polio. My father hadn't either. "We have enough trouble without polio," he signed when I asked him about it. "Maybe God has spared us."

But God did not spare Barry Goldstein, my friend from across the street. Late that summer, just as we were feeling the first hints of fall in the air and thinking that the danger might be over for the season, a blast of heat drove the cool air off. At the height of this last heat wave, Barry got sick. And his sickness became polio.

They took Barry to Coney Island Hospital, and he was immediately put into an iron lung. For the next few weeks, it was touch and go, but finally he stabilized. The iron lung did his breathing for him.

One day, Barry's father came to our apartment door with a handwritten note for my father: "You and Myron can visit my son if you want. I think he'd like that."

The very next Saturday, my father and I took the subway to Coney Island and walked to the hospital. My father did not direct a single sign to me. There was nothing he could say that would lessen my shock at Barry's illness and the sadness of his condition.

Coney Island Hospital seemed like the stuff of nightmares. We'd heard about people going there, but they never seemed to come out. We were sure it was the place where you went to die. Once my father and I arrived, the hospital's appearance more than lived up to my worst fears: dark hallways, cheerless gray rooms filled wall to wall with beds occupied by sad-looking sick people.

The elevator took us to the top floor, where we exited into a dark hallway. At the far end was a large room, blindingly illuminated by hanging lights. Inside were row upon row of iron lungs, in neat columns. Extending from the end of each one was a person's head, resting on a pillow. Above each head was a tilted mirror. By looking at this mirror, each head could see what was behind him or her. Looking in his mirror, Barry saw me. And looking in the same mirror, I saw Barry's upside-down face. He smiled at me, then looked at my father and smiled at him.

I told Barry about all that had been happening on the block since he had gotten sick. (I didn't once mention the word *polio*.) Some of the stories made him laugh. He told me I could use his bike until he came home and could use it himself. I nodded, not knowing what to say.

Soon a nurse came by and led us out, saying, "This boy needs his rest."

We said our goodbyes, and as I was leaving, Barry said, "You know, I have polio."

It was the terrible word that I had avoided mentioning, hoping deep down that if we avoided talking about Barry's condition, it wouldn't become reality. Probably, he would never walk again, I thought. And unless he got much better, he might never leave his iron lung. It wasn't just the summer days he would miss. He wouldn't graduate, go to college, get married, have children, or get a job. He would be trapped for life, forced to lie motionless, looking out at the world through a tiny mirror.

I wanted to cry. But I didn't want Barry to see me crying for him. I knew that would only make him feel worse.

Looking at my friend, helpless in the iron lung, I felt ashamed of myself. What did I have to complain about? Sure, my parents were deaf. They talked with their hands. They made funny noises when they tried to speak. They often embarrassed me to tears. Many times I wanted to shrivel up and disappear. Other times my skin burned at the attention I received, and it felt like it would peel off my body. But compared to Barry, and I figured a million other kids, my life looked pretty good.

On the way home in the subway car, my father signed to me his sadness. "Poor, poor boy."

But then he signed something surprising. "Now I know why I've never heard of a deaf person getting polio." He paused, thinking. "God wouldn't do that to a deaf person. How would a deaf person talk if his hands were hidden in an iron lung? How would a deaf person sign his fears with hidden hands?" My father did not sign another thought all the way home.

That fall, it rained almost every day. Barry's bike sat on his porch, exactly where he had left it after his last ride, a silent reminder of my friend. It was never taken in when it rained, and by the beginning of winter, it was covered in rust. With winter's first snowfall, it disappeared completely under a layer of snow.

But although I could no longer see Barry's red bike, its image under all that snow—with Barry, laughing like a madman, standing on the pedals, racing down our street—was engraved in my mind.

Now he was stuck in an iron lung, forced to wonder all day, "Why me?"

With that image, I thought of my father as a young boy Barry's age, deaf in the middle of a large, hearing family, living in a crowded neighborhood of hearing people, asking himself, "Why me?"

CHAPTER 23

A Boy Becomes a Man

On August 6, 1945, a single American plane dropped a single atomic bomb on the city of Hiroshima, Japan. In the days that followed, Japan, Italy, and Germany surrendered to the Allies, ending World War II.

One month earlier, the day after I turned twelve, my father had dropped a bomb on me. He told me I would have my bar mitzvah when I was thirteen. I couldn't believe it. Bar mitzvah? Since when, I wondered, was my father interested in the traditions of the Jewish religion? Until the day we visited Barry at the hospital, I had never really heard him talk about God or religion.

My father was born to Jewish parents, but he did not have a very religious upbringing. He'd had a bar mitzvah when he was thirteen, but it was more for show than anything. All he remembered of the event, he told me, was being dressed in a suit one Saturday and going with his father to the local storefront house of worship. There, he was pushed onto the wooden stage, where he stood with a shawl around his shoulders and a hat on his head. He watched carefully while the gray-bearded rabbi faced him, hair-covered lips moving a mile a minute.

"I had no idea," he told me, "what was going on. No one could explain it to me, and no one even bothered to try. Like much of my life in the hearing world at that age, nothing I experienced made much sense."

My grandfather thought that because his firstborn son could not hear, he could never truly participate in religious services. After all, in the Torah, Moses had told the priests to "Read it in their ears." Being deaf, how could my father hear the Torah? And because God did not speak in sign, how would God hear him respond?

175

So my father had his bar mitzvah in silence. It was all for show. The final thing my father told me about that day was that he saw tears falling from my grandfather's eyes. Tears of joy? Tears of sadness? My father could not say. But now, to the surprise of both sides of the family, my father was determined that his son, their firstborn grandchild, would have a bar mitzvah.

All the year that followed (I was sure it was the longest year of my life), I endured weekly bar mitzvah lessons. It was a dreary time filled with uncomprehending chanting done to the beat of the rabbi's rod on my desktop, with the occasional well-aimed swipe at my knuckles as I stumbled over a particularly difficult passage. For me, it was sheer torture.

But when I stood at the podium of our local synagogue reading my section of the Torah and reciting my "Today I Am a Man" speech, the look of pride on my father's face made the entire year of study worthwhile. His face was beaming up at me from the front row of the congregation, and his smile did not fade even though he could not hear a word I spoke. His hands never moved from his lap. But his face said it all. Just as his father had done so many years before, my father was quietly crying.

As for me, the bar mitzvah boy, the only result I experienced from my yearlong brush with religion was an amazing increase in speed. I could run like the wind. You see, as a "Jewish adult man" in the eyes of Jewish tradition, I was now eligible to complete the ten-man minyan. This was for the daily service at the synagogue, which often didn't attract the required minimum number of participants. So in the middle of a game played on our block, we would suddenly be interrupted by nine congregants sent out by the rabbi to search the neighborhood for a recent bar mitzvah boy. Since he was now a "man," he could complete the minyan, and I became their latest target.

I could almost hear the excited whispers of the Jewish men, older in years but still surprisingly fast, when they locked eyes on me: the newly minted bar mitzvah boy. Once they found me, I took off running.

My head start of a few yards was always enough as my sneakered feet pounded up the block, a gaggle of flapping long black coats in hot pursuit. And after a number of failed attempts, they focused their raids on newer, and slower, bar mitzvah boys.

As far as my father was concerned, other than the day of my bar mitzvah, it seemed as though my status had not changed. Most of the time, he still treated me as his child—that is, until we encountered a hearing-deaf situation. At these times, as so many times before, I was suddenly thrown into the role of adult, only to snap back into the role of child once my father's needs had been met.

It was a dizzying trick going from child to adult and back to child—a high-wire act that I could never look down from, for fear of falling. And nothing about it was made easier by the fact that I was now a *man*, the rabbi having said so.

CHAPTER 24

Sounds from the Heart

Of course, the rabbi was not quite right. And in no time at all, my newfound status as an adult was put to a serious test.

It was early evening, and I was waiting for my father to finish his bath before my mother came home. She had gone to Coney Island to visit her mother and sister. As I played with my newspaper hat and tried to make one for my brother, a scream shot into my ear and went straight to my heart.

It was coming from my father, and his deaf voice shattered the heavy stillness of our usually quiet apartment. He screamed again and again, the screams colliding with each other, bouncing off the tile walls of our small bathroom until they were one huge, all-enveloping sound of pain. I thought he was dying.

I shot to my feet and ran to my father, who was lying in the tub, covered in blood. He had dropped a glass shampoo bottle as he was getting out of the tub. And when he had reached to pick it up, he'd slipped and fallen onto the jagged fragments. Blood was pouring from a deep cut on his arm, and wherever I looked, I saw his bright-red blood coating the white tile surface of the room.

With one hand my father gripped his arm, trying to stop the flow of blood. With his other hand he signed for me to get the towel, his every movement flinging blood from his wound. I understood, and wrapped the towel as tightly as I could around his arm. My father then gathered the ends of the towel and twisted them into a loose knot to slow his loss of blood. My brother stood at the bathroom door, watching in horror.

Furiously, I stomped my feet on the bathroom floor. Our neighbor below recognized immediately that this was our agreed-upon signal of emergency and not the usual foot stamping our deaf family used to gain each other's attention. An ambulance soon arrived. I went with my father to serve as his translator, and I brought my brother with us. I was afraid that if left him alone in our empty apartment, he might have a seizure from the excitement.

The emergency attendant who cared for my father's wound on the way to Coney Island Hospital directed all his questions to me as soon as he understood that my father was deaf.

"How did this happen?" he asked me in the back of the ambulance as we careened around corners and sped down the streets of Brooklyn.

I asked my father.

"He slipped in the bathtub and fell on broken glass," I interpreted.

"Ask your father how much blood he's lost."

I asked my father.

"How should I know?" he answered me with one hand, while holding on to the blood-drenched towel with the other. "Is this guy an idiot?"

"A lot," I told the attendant.

"Ask your father what his blood type is."

I asked my father.

"This guy *is* an idiot," my father responded with disgust.

"My father wants to know, what are the choices?"

"A, B, or O," the attendant said.

I told my father his choices.

"It's all alphabet soup to me," my father signed. "Just get me to a doctor!"

"He's not sure," I said.

We arrived at the emergency entrance of the hospital, and I was asked to go to the admissions office while my father was rushed into the emergency room.

For more than an hour, I tried to answer all the questions they asked about my father.

"Is your father deaf?"

"Yes."

"Can he hear if we speak loudly?"

"No, he is deaf."

"Can he hear if we shout?"

I didn't bother answering. I had received this question constantly when in public with my father. When I answered, "No, he is deaf," hearing people would often then shout at him over and over. When he didn't respond, they would walk off in disgust.

"Where does your father work? Does he have insurance? Do you have a telephone? Do you have a mother? Is she deaf? What's her name? How can we reach her?"

On and on it went. I answered as best I could.

"How come you can hear?"

I couldn't understand what that had to do with anything.

"How old are you?"

That one I answered with no problem.

After the skin had been sewn back to my father's arm with enough stitches to remind me of my model train tracks, and he had received a transfusion of two pints of blood, I spoke to my father's doctor. Or actually, he spoke to me.

"Tell your father he's lost a great deal of blood," the doctor said.

"Brilliant man," my father signed, his damaged arm thickly wrapped in gauze and tape from wrist to elbow.

"My father says 'Thank you' for advising him of that fact."

"Tell your father he has to keep his arm dry for the

next week, change the dressing twice a day, and apply ointment each time he changes the bandages. I will give you a prescription for the ointment. Tell the pharmacist you want the ointment in a tube, not in a jar. Tell your father he must drink at least eight glasses of water a day, and he should eat lots of meat, like calf's liver, as he is anemic from the loss of blood."

While the doctor was telling me all of this, my father was watching the doctor's mouth with growing anxiety.

"What did the doctor say?" he kept interrupting.

"Later," I answered. "I'll tell you later."

"No! Tell me now! I'm not a child!" My father flung angry signs at me, accompanied by his harsh voice.

The people in the hospital corridor stared with rude fascination at my father and his excited signing. Others looked on in disgust and cringed at his voice, which reverberated down the hallway, stopping people in their tracks.

With my brother at my side, I wanted to shout at them, "What are you looking at? We're not freaks."

My father saw my eyes drift away from his and understood what he read in my face.

"Pay no attention to the hearing people," he practically shouted at me in sign. "They are stupid. They don't know better. They don't know our deaf ways."

As I began to explain to my father what the doctor had said, the doctor interrupted me, saying, "I'm quite busy. I can't spend more time with your father. Tell him—"

My father pulled my arm. "What is the doctor saying?" His signs screeched across my mind like the sound of chalk scratching on a blackboard.

I begged the doctor to be patient with my father. I asked my father to be patient with me. I told my brother that our father would be all right. And my head began to throb with a headache.

Eventually, I had transmitted all the necessary instructions from the doctor to my father, my father's many questions to the doctor, and the doctor's abrupt answers to my father in highly edited form.

Finally, my father was satisfied, and we went home.

I sat between my father and my brother in the subway car, the three of us leaning in to one another, away from the other passengers. I answered as best I could the other questions my father had. My brother had no questions to ask me. He was simply grateful to be going home.

Suddenly, my father took me in his arms and then said, "I'm sorry I need you to be my voice in the hearing world. Especially when there is a big emergency." He looked deeply into my eyes and told me he loved me, and that he was proud of me. His sign for proud was expansive. His thumb rose against his chest, tracing a passage from waist to neck, while his chest expanded with pride.

I was surprised to hear my father say this. Usually, he acted as if translating was my expected role in life. The instant the occasion arose, I would switch from being his son to his interpreter. And when we were done, I switched back. But this had been a life-and-death experience. Today he needed me for much more than "What did he say?"

Maybe the rabbi was right after all. I felt older that day.

CHAPTER 25

Dad, Jackie, and Me

With the summer of 1947 came a special, once-in-a-lifetime opportunity for me. Shortly after my fourteenth birthday, my father gave me a belated present. Coming home from work one night, a wide grin on his face, he held up two tickets. Sign was unnecessary.

My father had never had much interest in sports, except the occasional boxing match. But that spring everything had changed when the Brooklyn Dodgers signed Jackie Robinson. Jackie was the first black man to play in major league baseball.

The United States had just won a world war against an enemy that thought their race, the Aryan race, was superior to all others. Yet in America, segregation was still practiced in many areas of life. Major league baseball was segregated, meaning only white baseball players were allowed to play. But with us winning the war, it felt like a new world now, and a black man was playing first base for our home team. Who would have thought it possible?

My father put down the newspaper he had been reading and handed me the precious pair of thick cardboard tickets. In bold black letters, the tickets announced, "Brooklyn Dodgers vs. St. Louis Cardinals." In Brooklyn, we hated the Cards with such passion that the words might as well have been "Brooklyn Goes to War."

My father took up a batter's stance and wagged an invisible bat menacingly over his shoulder, his eyes squinting, the better to see the arrival over the plate of an invisible spinning baseball, which he appeared completely capable of smashing out of the park.

As much as I couldn't wait to see the Dodgers play, something didn't add up. I simply could not understand my father's sudden interest in Jackie Robinson. I knew my father's history well because he enjoyed telling me stories about when he was my age, and I knew that as a boy in a deaf military academy, he hadn't had many opportunities for play of any kind, including sports.

First he had to learn discipline, for at that time deaf children were thought by their hearing teachers to be uncontrollable animals. Then he had to be taught the basics of reading and writing—a difficult process for the teachers, and a grueling one for the students. Play was something available only to the hearing kids, the teachers at his school had said.

Baffled as I was, I certainly didn't let this get in the way of my excitement. I had never been to Ebbets Field and had never seen the Dodgers play. I knew this was going to be the highlight of the summer.

I was an overnight sensation on my block when I showed my friends—but did not allow them to touch—the tickets. I slept with the tickets under my pillow at night and never let them out of my sight during daylight hours.

Finally, the big day arrived. I gazed up at the entrance of Ebbets Field in awe. The elegant curve of the rotunda drew us into that hallowed place. Once through the clacking wooden turnstile, clutching our ticket stubs for dear life, we joined the excited mob walking up the dimly lit stone ramp beneath the towering concrete ceiling. We then exited out a small doorway into an arena overlooking a field of impossibly green grass, which was split by perfectly groomed brown base paths and bordered by strictly drawn powdered white lines. The whole scene sparkled like a polished diamond in the summer sunlight.

So this is what it looks like in real life, I thought.

Like every other kid in my neighborhood, I had listened on the radio to Red Barber announce every single Dodgers game of the season. I could not walk down my block without hearing the Old Redhead calling out balls and strikes from every open window. I now realized that the images I had created in my mind from listening to the radio were nothing more than black-and-white silhouettes. *This* magnificent sight was in living color.

Our seats were perfect. Box seats right on the first-base line, fifty feet from Jackie Robinson himself. Jackie made his presence known in the third inning. He smacked a double off the left field wall, sending the runner home for the first run.

The game quickly turned into a pitching duel that would last until the Cards tied the score late in the game. It was going to come down to the wire. Inning after inning, play after play, my father showered me with questions. With one eye on the action and the other on him, I tried my best to describe as quickly as possible the significance of all that was happening on the field. Of course, up until that time I had never actually *seen* a professional baseball game, but having listened to Red Barber, I felt I was an expert.

Then the unthinkable happened. A Cardinals batter racing down the first-base line in an impossible attempt to beat out a ground ball reached out with his leg and drove his spiked cleats into Jackie's leg. It was long after the ball had arrived in Jackie's glove, and it was clear the runner had done it on purpose. The steel spikes on baseball cleats were long and sharp to allow the players to grip the turf and dirt. Jackie's leg immediately started to bleed.

Twenty-six thousand Brooklyn fans leaped to their feet, and the stands erupted in protest. Cries of outrage poured from twenty-six thousand mouths, swirled up the aisles, bounced off the girders, and reverberated against the roof.

"JACKIEE! JACKIEE! JACKIEE!" they screamed.

My father's shouts of "AH-GHEE! AH-GHEE! AH-GHEE!" went unheard in the flood of sound.

Jackie Robinson simply stood on first base. Bright-red blood was streaming down his leg. His face looked as if it had been carved in marble, like a statue. Jackie would not give the other team the satisfaction of seeing that he was hurt.

Later in the game, Jackie got a hit off the Cardinals pitcher. Again, the fans went crazy.

"JACKIEE! JACKIEE! JACKIEE!"

"AH-GHEE! AH-GHEE! AH-GHEE!"

This time, the fans in the neighboring seats looked at my father. I was almost positive my father knew they were staring at him, but he kept his eyes locked on Jackie, who was beginning to edge off second base. I looked at my feet.

On the subway ride home, my father signed, "I am a deaf man in a hearing world. All the time, I must show hearing people that I am a man as well. A man as good as them. Maybe even better."

The subway car was packed. As usual, people in the car stared at my father with mixed looks of curiosity, shock, and even disgust. I paid no attention to them as I watched his hands.

"Jackie Robinson is a black man in the white man's baseball world. All the time, he must show white people that he is a man. A man as good as them. Maybe even better. No matter that his skin is a black color. The color of his skin is not important. Only what Jackie does on the ball field is important."

Just when I thought my father had finished speaking, his hands spoke to me sadly, "Very hard for a deaf man. Very hard for a black man. Must fight all the time. No rest. *Never*. Sad."

My father didn't sign another word. He just stared into the eyes of the subway riders looking at him, until they sheepishly broke off eye contact—every last one of them.

We went to many more home games during that summer. Somehow, my father always got box seat tickets along the first-base line. And at each game, his voice rang out proudly, with perfect clarity, "AH-GHEE! AH-GHEE! AH-GHEE!"

CHAPTER 26

Silent Snow

The summer of 1947 saw a black man play baseball in Ebbets Field for the Brooklyn Dodgers. And at the end of that year, I witnessed another incredible event in the history of our borough, the sight of Ebbets Field covered under piles of snow.

On a night in December, I was awakened by a profound silence, a total absence of sound of any kind. It was like my bedroom was smothered by a giant down-filled pillow. It was a silence that had weight. A silence that filled our small apartment like water in a fish tank.

Living in our third-floor apartment, there was always some kind of noise coming from outside. During the day, the sounds of children playing, and adults gossiping and arguing and complaining, drifted up to my open bedroom window. At night, the children safely in bed, the adults hit the street below my window to continue their gossiping and arguing and complaining in their distinctive Brooklyn voices. But not this night. I went to my window and saw something remarkably different, an impenetrable white wall of falling snow.

We expected some snow in our neighborhood, but what I was looking at was unheard of. Some twenty hours later, it would be recorded as the greatest snow-fall in the history of Brooklyn—exceeding even the legendary record-setting Blizzard of 1888 by more than five inches.

In that dead silence, while my brother was still asleep, I heard the sound of my father muttering in his sleep. Looking into his room, I saw him tossing and turning, locked in a dream that would not let him go. But the strange thing was that his hands were signing his dream for me to see. I had never seen him do this before, but then again, I was in the habit of letting my parents sleep undisturbed—unless there was a fox in our apartment, that is.

The next morning, with all of us kept at home by the new-fallen snow, I asked my father if he dreamed in sign.

"I don't know," he said. "I never thought to wonder."

"Do you think in sign?" I asked.

"I'm not sure," he answered. "All my thinking comes at once. Sometimes I see a complete picture in my head."

Then he hesitated. "Wait. That's not all true. Sometimes I think about a problem with sign pictures. Also, sometimes I talk out my thinking to myself with my hands. My language is in my hands. My memories are in my hands. All my thinking is in my hands."

Then my father's hands told me a story:

"When I was a young man in the big Depression, I knew a deaf boy who worked in a dangerous factory. He had no choice. He had to bring his family some money to buy food to eat. There were many people in his family and his father was dead, so the boy had to be the father.

"The deaf boy worked six days a week, twelve hours a day. He got very tired. One day, he was so tired he did not pay close attention to the machine he was working on, and the machine took off the fingers of his right hand. All the fingers. After his hand healed, the deaf boy lost his language. He could only talk with one hand. Deaf people did not clearly understand him. Very sad. Now I have nightmares of this bad thing happening to me."

My father stopped signing and stared at his hands.

"How would I talk if such a terrible thing happened to me?" he signed. "My language is in my hands. How would I tell of my love for my beautiful Sarah? And if I had no hands, how would I touch and hold my boys?"

I realized then my father loved his language. To him, it was more than just a tool for communication. He told me sign was part of him. There was not a single thought or an emotion he felt that he could not express to the fullest, in sign language—even his dreams.

I also realized something about myself. I realized that my father appreciated my ability to sign—that ability brought us together—but I also knew he was disappointed that I would never be fluent. I knew enough to communicate with my father, but not enough to dream with him.

As I watched my father tell me this story, I realized I would never be fully in my parents' world. I was like a close planet in tight orbit. I knew that they loved me, but I was different because I could hear. My father's hearing parents and siblings were in orbits farther out. As were his neighbors, then fellow workers. And finally, like all the visible but distant stars in the universe, there existed a vast multitude of hearing people that my parents could never possibly know.

My father and I looked with wonder out our apartment window at the snow piled deeply in front of the downstairs entrance to our apartment building. Nothing was moving on our block. Nothing was visible—no blacktop street, no sewers, no curb, no fire hydrant, no iron picket fence, no garbage cans, no stoop, no cars—but here and there were occasional humps in the snow blanket, shadowy shapes that suggested what lay beneath.

"It's very quiet," I signed.

"Sure is," he responded. Then he smiled. "Let's go down and see how it feels, not sounds."

By now, my brother had joined us at the window. His

eyes were as wide as the sewer covers now buried under the snow.

"Watch what else my hands can do," my father signed. He grabbed a snow shovel with one hand and my sled in the other. While I held on to my brother's hand, we marched out of our apartment, down the stairs, and out into, what seemed to my brother and me, the North Pole.

CHAPTER 27

My Brother's Keeper

In 1947, my brother turned ten, and just as quickly as his seizures had begun five years earlier, they suddenly came to a stop. Finally, he was relieved of his daily torture: the bruises from his falls, the swollen, bitten tongue, the chipped teeth, and the headaches that lasted for hours.

Maybe most important of all, he could stop taking his medication, which had helped control his epilepsy but had limited him in other ways. The daily dosage had often left him confused and so tired that he looked like he was sleepwalking.

Fortunately, he was never held back in school. But this, of course, created other problems. Since there was no way Irwin could keep up with his schoolwork, his teachers often sent him home early with handwritten notes asking my father to come in for a conference. These requests meant that my father had to get a half day off from work and that I had to get permission to skip a half day of school.

Before each of the meetings, my father insisted that we bring my brother to the doctor to get a professional opinion of his ability to do the work. At the doctor's office, I interpreted for my father the doctor's assessment of what could be expected of my brother, and all the medical reasons for those expectations. Then I interpreted my father's questions in response. The delayed back-and-forth soon became frustrating for both of them.

Not helping matters, the nurse kept popping in to announce that the waiting room was full, and that the doctor's patients were threatening to find another doctor, one who was not so busy. Of course, I interpreted this for my father as well.

"So tell her to tell those idiots to get another doctor," my father instructed me. Whether he was serious or not, I never knew. But to keep him happy, I silently mouthed some nonsense in the general direction of the nurse as she left the office. This way, I figured, my father would think I passed on his message, and no one would be offended.

All the while, my brother looked at me nervously, waiting for me to explain what was going on, and, I thought, to speak up for him. In these situations, with both the doctor and my father needing my attention and my translations, I was hard-pressed to take the time to give my brother the reassurance I could tell he needed.

As I'd gotten older, my resentment of my brother's need of me had faded. He tried so hard to be just like the other kids on our street. But he had always been trapped between seizure and recovery, and much of the time he was numb from the medications he needed to take.

Now the epilepsy had loosened its grip on him. And soon he stopped taking most of his medications. He gained some confidence and picked up a hobby of his own: roller-skating. Slowly at first, then with growing confidence, he began skating around our neighborhood. At first, he could barely navigate on wobbly ankles the length of our block. But eventually he skated around our block—up Ninth Street to Avenue P, around the corner, down Tenth Street to Stillwell Avenue, and back to our apartment building on Ninth Street.

Then he went even farther, skating from our block to Coney Island, three miles away, and then back again. He always skated alone. It seemed like he wanted to prove to me that he could do things on his own.

At the meetings with our family doctor, and then with his teachers, I would tell them about his new skill, hoping they would see it as evidence he could keep up with his schoolwork, even though I wasn't really sure this was the case.

At the doctor's office, my efforts seemed to be convincing. After talking to all of us and doing seemingly endless tests on my brother to determine his mental abilities, the doctor always instructed me: "Tell your father that with extra attention, your brother can at least keep up with his grade level."

After our visit to the doctor, we headed to my brother's school, where I resumed my back-and-forth ping-pong of translating. Round after round of meetings followed.

And at every meeting, the same question came up: "Who will be responsible for helping the boy keep up with his classmates?"

Silence. Much looking at each other. Much wise nodding of our heads. "Who will be providing the extra hours of work explaining the boy's homework to him?"

Continued silence. Eye-avoiding looks. Heads bobbing. "And who will be monitoring his progress on a daily basis?"

I interpreted each of the teachers' questions for my father.

"Well?" the teachers demanded, looking at my father for the first time during the conversation. Normally, in these types of interactions, the hearing person never looked at my father, just at me. As for my father, to them he might as well have been a tree stump.

"Well..." my father hesitantly signed, staring helplessly back at the teachers, the size of the task overwhelming him.

My brother, knowing that he was the focus of this back-and-forth exercise, looked at both, while they, in turn, looked back at him.

Then, as one, they all looked at me.

Hide-and-go-seek was one of my favorite games, and

it was wildly popular in our neighborhood. Its rules were simple. To begin the game, one unlucky person was designated as It. The kid so identified would remain It, until he (the girls in our neighborhood had no interest in this game) succeeded in tagging another unlucky kid, while shouting, "You're It." And so the game continued with kids becoming It and then passing It to someone else, until we were too tired or bored to play any longer.

Hide-and-go-seek was one of our simpler games. You didn't need a bat or a ball or a glove to play it. The thing that made it work was that every kid, without fail, absolutely dreaded being It. Being It meant that everyone was watching you, and nobody wanted to be near you. The game continued because every time a new person became It, he would do anything to be rid of the role as fast as possible, to pass it on to someone else. The good thing about the game was that there always *was* someone else.

I loved playing hide-and-go-seek, and when my turn came, I didn't mind at all the brief time I spent being It. But now as I sat still in that room, as everyone stared at me, the teachers' question hanging in the air unanswered,

I realized that I was It. And there was no one else I could pass that role to.

As I nodded my acceptance, I swore to myself that one day, someday, I would be rid of this obligation, to both my deaf parents and my sick brother. I had my own life to live. And my own world to live it in.

I didn't know when that day might come, but I knew somehow that it was out there waiting for me.

CHAPTER 28

Pigskin Dreams

Being deaf had kept my father sidelined as a child from many of the games and activities the other kids, including his brother and sisters, enjoyed. And from early in my life, he had seemed determined that I would have the childhood activities he never did.

When I was little, he bought me an authentic leather Wilson football. It was way too big for me to grip in my tiny hands, and my mother told him it was too early for me to get into sports. But my father did not budge. "He will grow," he signed to her. His sign for *grow* started with his closed right hand appearing ever so slowly from behind his open left hand. Rising upward, it grew, spreading wide, flushed with new life. As I watched, the petals of the blooming plant unfolded, and the stalk of his right arm rose ever higher, seeking the warmth of the sun. Then, so there was no doubt about how big I'd be one day, he held his right hand, palm down at his waist, and slowly raised it until it was over his head—and he smiled.

I had tried to imagine myself someday as strong as he was, and even taller. I hadn't thought it was possible. I'd been more fascinated by my father's signs than I had been with the big, clumsy football, which I had forgotten all about.

But I did grow. First, it had seemed to me that my feet were the only thing getting bigger. Then in time, my hands caught up. But the rest of my body—in between my feet and my hands—not so much. For a very scary while, my imagination going full blast, I had imagined what I would look like if this kept up until I hit high school. I'd be the laughingstock of the school, and I knew how that felt.

But one day, overnight it seemed, the rest of my body had gotten the message from my feet and my hands and done what Mother Nature promised, and my science teacher had said would happen—and I grew, putting on weight and height.

As I'd grown, with my father's encouragement, I played all the street games with the kids on my block. They were the same games that were played by kids on every block in every neighborhood of Brooklyn. But unlike my friends' fathers, who were usually too tired after a day's work, or too concerned with the lengthening reach of the Depression, my father had always watched our street games. And he'd become my greatest fan.

He would stand on the curb, which was the sideline of our football field and the third-base line of our stickball games. Our playing field was not covered in the soft green grass of a real football field but in solid black pavement, interrupted by the occasional manhole cover. It was not the most comfortable surface to slide on or fall on.

And yet, I had fallen and slid, and each fall and slide had been accompanied by my father's deaf voice shouting encouragement. "Great catch!" "You're safe!" My friends could make no sense of these harsh sounds, but I under-stood them, and they had been the unremarked-upon soundtrack to many of our games.

One day, I'd run into a parked car while reaching for a winning touchdown pass. My last conscious thought was that I had my man beat and would score easily. I'd woken up in Coney Island Hospital. The first person I saw was my father sitting beside my bed. "You scored," he signed. Then he added, "Now what the heck will we tell Mother?"

—————

Now I was sixteen. And it was time for me to try out for a real team. I reported to football tryouts one late-summer day on our high school field. The field, like our school, was new—so not even a single blade of grass had grown on its surface. But it did not lack other objects, most noticeably, rocks. These rocks, randomly seeded, were hard, but I figured this field could not be any harder than the pavement where I'd learned to play the game.

My father had been urging me to go out for football, but I wasn't so sure I was ready. As I looked in my bathroom mirror every day, flexing my skinny arms, while puffing out my still-hairless chest, I looked kind of scrawny. No matter how much I held my breath, tensed my biceps, strained and struggled, grunted and groaned, not much happened. The kid in the mirror was still the same old me.

However, I thought, *I may be on the small side, but I'm fast, and I'm determined.*

The coach presiding over the tryouts was Harry Ostro, who had served with the 101st Airborne Division in World War II. Ostro had been a paratrooper in the largest airborne battle in history, Operation Market Garden. After successfully leading his platoon inside enemy lines, Ostro had been seriously wounded. But all I knew about him at the time, and only because it was very obvious, was that he had a metal plate in his head—something he never spoke about. The coach was the toughest man I had ever met. He didn't talk. He growled.

The tryout was brutal. And it soon became clear that I did not exactly measure up to the other players in terms of skill. But what I could do was withstand the grueling physical and mental test that Coach Ostro put us through. And that was apparently enough for me to earn a spot on the team.

High school was a new world for me. A mile from my apartment building, it was much farther away than my middle school had been. Most importantly, there were many more kids in high school. And, of course, they were all bigger and older than I was.

The good thing, at least to me, was that they were all strangers. They didn't know me, or my deaf patents—and they had never seen my brother have an epileptic fit. I would be safe, I hoped, from the unwanted attention I'd ended up getting in middle school—where, it seemed, *everyone* found out that I was the son of deaf parents. Here was another chance to be just another kid in the midst of a thousand others. This was a big school, four floors high, and a full block in size. No one would notice me here, I thought. I'd be invisible.

But my inconspicuousness did not and could not last.

As my biggest supporter, my father came to every one of my football games. At every football field in Brooklyn. He was determined not to miss seeing me play, on the off chance that I actually got into a game. Thankfully, there was little chance of me getting in the game unless we were up by a hundred points, something that I had never known to happen. I figured that by staying off the field I would be safe from the attention of the crowd.

I was wrong.

Although I rode the bench as a lowly sub, my father became a football fanatic and a loyal superfan of Lafayette High School. That was the name of my school, and when he screamed, as he seemed to do on every play—"Go, Lafayette!"—the sound of his voice cut through the general fog of sound that surrounded every game. But when he screamed in an extra-high pitch, "Put Uhlberg in the game!" I thought I'd die. Every eye on our bench turned to me. I stared down at my football cleats, mortified.

But over time, just as had happened on my street, my father's voice seemed to fade into the general noise of the crowd, and the sound again became just another part of the game. My teammates also got used to my father, just as my friends on the block had. And they started to appreciate him for being such a loyal fan of our team.

Before long, I began to feel like I belonged on the high school team, and after my first season, I was awarded a football letter, which my mother sewed onto my varsity sweater. I wore that sweater until it was in tatters.

The following year, I grew two inches and added twenty pounds to my scrawny frame. Apparently, this was enough for Coach Ostro to feel confident using me in games. At least, he must have figured, I wouldn't be killed.

My father came to every game, as usual, and we would spend the evening after the game analyzing the good and bad plays. My father had learned much about the game by watching me play. But we had to create a whole new vocabulary of signs to describe the details of the game.

Usually signs are a combination of hand shapes and movements that represent the thing being signed. Other times, signs can have little resemblance to the word or action. These signs are harder to pick up because the connection to their meaning is not as clear. But with use, like all signs, they become part of your vocabulary. Now that I was a football player, my father became a student of signs and, after every game, invented a new sign that represented some extraordinary action that had happened that day.

The season progressed with me playing here and there. But the night before our final game of the season, disaster struck the team. Our star tailback fell down a flight of stairs and landed, right hand extended, on broken glass. The next afternoon, he showed up at the field of our archrivals, New Utrecht High School, with his arm heavily bandaged. He could not suit up. The team was in a state of shock. Joe Darienzo was a senior. This was supposed to be his last game. He was Brooklyn's best tail-back and the leader of our team. A genuine triple-threat, he could run, pass, and kick. We all sat there in the locker room before the opening kickoff, dejected and with a sense of impending doom.

The coach stood with his arm draped over Joe's shoulder and addressed the team.

"Men, this is the most important game of the season."

We knew that.

"Joe wanted more than anything to play this game. But he can't."

We knew that.

"Joe is an important part of this team. But it is the *team* that wins, or loses, not any single man."

We knew that.

"As a *team*, we can win this game today."

We weren't at all sure of that.

215

Then he told us that I would start in Joe's place.

I didn't know that. The team didn't know that. My father didn't know that. But when he saw me in the backfield on the very first play, he knew that this would be a memorable game. And he began to dream up new football signs, since we would have much to discuss that evening.

How much, I had no idea, as I stood in a daze, waiting to receive the opening hike from our center. He was looking back at me, upside down between his legs, with obvious skepticism on his face. His look did little to assure me. The rest of the game passed in a blur. The only solid memory I have is being yelled at. The coach yelled at me. Joe, overcoat slung over his shoulder and arm in a sling, yelled at me. My father, who had been given a sideline pass for the game, yelled at me, as he relentlessly recorded my every mistake on his windup movie camera.

The tailback on our team was the most important position. I was the one who took the snap and handled the ball on every play. Every eye in the stadium was on me. And me, what did I do? Well, every pass I threw was a picture-perfect spiral…right into the hands of a waiting defender. Every run I made…was stopped at the line of scrimmage. Every handoff I attempted was bobbled or fumbled. I was a disaster.

However, my teammates played an extraordinary game, more than making up for my mistakes, and we were tied in the final quarter. Then in the final minutes, our coach came up with a desperation play, an all-or-nothing shot at winning. It was based on the assumption that, given my pathetic performance all that long afternoon, nobody on the opposing team would be paying me much attention.

As a threat, I was about as dangerous as our head cheerleader. So no one would wonder why the hike from center, rather than going to me, as was normal, went to our fullback to my right. Exaggerating the fact that I was empty-handed, I veered to the left. (Being good at sign language, I was a decent actor, and finally I had a role on this miserable afternoon that I could fill.)

Meanwhile, the fullback made a big show of handing the ball off to Tommy LaSpada, who was headed in the other direction.

While this dumb show was playing itself out in the backfield, our linemen went into a choreographed ballet, feinting this way and that, confusing not only the opposing team but themselves as well.

In the midst of all the hullabaloo, I calmly drifted back to my right, and Tommy, coming from the other direction, handed the ball to me so slyly that the oncoming defender missed the move. One look at the fierce expression on the defender's face, and Tommy realized he was going to be crushed to the ground. Tommy, although tough, was one of the smallest members of the team— and he was no fool. I heard Tommy scream, "I don't have the ball!" And that was my signal to get out of there fast.

Our cartoon play had been so successful that no one was watching me—and I ran for my life down the right sideline, unnoticed and untouched, scoring a touchdown. We had won the game, just as our coach had said we would, and the crowd went wild. But through all the sound, I could clearly make out my father's whooping voice.

That evening, he laughingly taught me the strangest made-up signs I would ever learn in my lifetime.

CHAPTER 29

Exodus

During my senior year in high school I was offered a football scholarship to Brandeis University, a brand-new school in New England that had sophomore, junior, and senior classes but needed a freshman class. They also needed football players who would be willing to take the chance of going to a school that wouldn't even be eligible for certification for another two years.

I had also been offered a football scholarship to New York University—but their campus was in the Bronx, and if I accepted that offer, it would mean continuing to live at home and going to school by subway. I never considered it for a moment.

My father was ecstatic for me. I would be the first on both sides of my family to go to college.

"You must look like a college man," he signed. "I don't want them to think you're a yokel from the sticks."

Brooklyn? I wondered. *The sticks?* But I didn't argue. Going to college was going to be as exciting an experience for him as it would be for me. And I wouldn't deny him the pleasure of dressing me up like a college man. Our once-a-year trips to Mr. Bloomingdale, and to Mr. R. and H. Macy, became an almost weekly ritual the summer after my senior year. With photos of college men torn out of magazines clutched in his hands, my father and I scoured the racks of suits with me to find those that would make me look the part and—more importantly—would last for four years. Now I didn't mind at all the attention we received. It actually felt good.

Finally, one day in early August, my father came with me to Grand Central Station, where I would catch the train to Boston. I was dressed in a heavy wool suit. It was about 90 degrees in the station, but I didn't sign one word of complaint. As the conductor shouted, "All aboard!" my father looked me over one last time and signed, "You look like a college man, for sure." Then he added, "I'll see you soon."

Little did I know at the time how true that would be. He came to every home football game we played for the next four years, always carrying a heavy cardboard care package my mother had spent all week preparing. The packages contained food she felt was unavailable in Boston and that without which, she believed, I would starve to death.

In carefully constructed compartments were a ten-inch kosher salami; a jar of matzo ball soup; another of chicken soup (so I wouldn't catch a cold); a freshly baked loaf of rye bread; one homemade challah; enormous spicy pickles; a large jar of pickled herring; chicken legs and drumsticks; small cakes and oatmeal cookies; and napkins.

In four years at college, I never caught a cold, and I certainly did not starve to death, both facts that made my mother very happy.

Stepping onto the train that day, I took the final step, the step from my parents' world to living in my own.

From then on, when I was with my parents, I would only be a visitor to our silent world. It had been a world of great beauty filled with limitless love, but also frequent shame. It was also a difficult world where I had been asked to play the role of an adult.

In sign, the gesture for *responsibility* is a dramatic one. It was one of the first signs my father taught me. He would place both hands on his right shoulder with his fingertips pushing down hard. His shoulder would slump, as if it was carrying a heavy load, and his face took on a look of patient endurance. This is what was always expected of me: to be responsible—for my father and his needs, and then when my brother became sick, for my brother too. There were times when I found the weight to be crushing, and those were the days when I would rush from my apartment to the roof of our building and hide for hours on end.

Now, as I sat on the cushioned seat of the railroad car directly over the iron wheels that carried me away with each revolution from the only home I had ever known, I felt that weight lifting.

But there was also another feeling that came with this

CHAPTER 30

The Duke of Coney Island

My uncle David was my mother's favorite brother. He is a magician, a sorcerer, she always said. David was a sorcerer to my mother because with a wink of his brown eyes, he could transform her sadness into joy. Every other member of her family made my mother feel different, but David acted as though my mother's deafness was nothing more important, or significant, than the color of her eyes or the texture of her hair. Everyone in my mother's family, as well as all of his many friends, called David the Duke of Coney Island because of his suave new freedom—a sense of loss. My time living with them was over. I would still be their son, and my brother's brother, but my world had gotten bigger, and theirs was still the same. I had gone forward, and they were now left behind.

In all the days I had dreamed about being free from the responsibility of my parents, it had never occurred to me that I might feel this way.

manner and elegant clothes, and because he managed both of these things without having a steady job.

To me, David was a wizard. He could do magic tricks—wondrous, surpassingly amazing sleight-of-hand stunts that left me gasping.

When I turned six, he began the ritual of pulling objects from my ear on every birthday. That year it was a penny. When I turned seven, it was a nickel. At eight, he produced a dime. And at nine, a quarter. The following year it was a half dollar.

The year I turned eleven, my uncle David, after much hocus-pocus, rolled up the sleeve of his right arm and, with great exaggeration, displayed his empty hand under my nose. Wiggling his five fingers in the air, he proceeded with incredible slowness to curl his middle finger, then the finger to its left, and finally his pinkie into a ball. With the remaining forefinger and thumb, he formed a claw.

Slowly, he moved the claw to my ear, then into my ear, and with much grunting and twisting, he extracted a giant, gleaming silver dollar. It was magnificent.

Placing the silver dollar on its edge, with a twist of his fingers, he set it spinning on a nearby surface. "This coin reminds me of you," he said before the coin came to a stop. I nodded solemnly. I didn't have a clue what he meant.

I didn't find out until years later, when we were both living in Los Angeles and I was riding in a car with him. He asked me if I remembered my eleventh birthday and the silver dollar he had pulled from my ear.

When I was young, David said, I always seemed to him to be two sides of the same coin, both one thing and its opposite. I was split into two parts, half hearing, half deaf, forever joined together. And he had seen me wobble and vibrate between being the child that my age indicated and the adult I was forced to be in thought and action. When my uncle looked at me, he saw that I stood at the crossroads of sound and silence, of childhood and adulthood, and that I would have to struggle to find my own way.

With his explanation I realized how hard I had fought, all of my young life, to break free from my parents' need of me—particularly my father's. It was a struggle I kept up in order to feel as though I had a life of my own, that I was my own person. But it was a struggle I fought with one hand tied behind my back because I could never let my father think that I was abandoning him.

On that long ride I took with my uncle, I thought about the other side of my childhood's equation: my mother. Unlike my father, she asked only that I help her with the everyday interactions with the hearing world: What was the price of this? The availability of that?

I realized that the difference between my mother and father had to do with the fact that my mother had become deaf as an infant. She had no memory of sound. For her, sound was something she couldn't put her finger on, just an idea. Unlike my mother, my father had lost his hearing later in life. Until the age of three, he could hear. Somewhere, buried in his brain was the memory of sound. That memory would not release him, and through me, he seemed to try to find it.

My father needed me to help him remember sound. To understand sound itself. Sound in all its forms. Sound in all its versions. The shape and feeling of sound. Even the color of sound. In turn, I needed my father to appreciate the gift of sound. Along with sight, it completes me, turning a black-and-white world into color.

My father's questions began when I was six years old. They were questions I could never answer completely, and they did not stop until I left his deaf world forever, twelve years later, on my way to college.

Now, when I think of my father, and I remember the daily struggles of life in my parents' world, I often think of my uncle David's birthday gift: the silver dollar. Oh, how I wish I had saved it. I would set it spinning. What would it tell me now?

About the Author

Myron Uhlberg is the award-winning and critically acclaimed author of several books, including the picture books *Dad, Jackie, and Me*; *A Storm Called Katrina*; and *The Sound of All Things* as well as the adult memoir *Hands of My Father*, upon which *The Sound of Silence* is based.

He was born in Brooklyn, New York, and was the first-born son of two deaf parents. Upon graduating from Brandeis University, he enlisted in the US Army and served as a paratrooper. After spending thirty-five years in the fashion business and running twenty marathons in his spare time, he returned to his first love: writing books for young readers.

Myron lives in California, dividing his time between the beach of Santa Monica and the desert of Palm Springs.

100 Years of

Albert Whitman & Company

1919–2019

Albert Whitman & Company encompasses all ages and reading levels, including board books, picture books, early readers, chapter books, middle grade, and YA

Present

2017

The Boxcar Children celebrates its 75th anniversary and the second Boxcar Children movie, *Surprise Island*, is scheduled to be released

2014

The first Boxcar Children movie is released

2008

John Quattrocchi and employee Pat McPartland buy Albert Whitman & Company, continuing the tradition of keeping it independently owned and operated

1989

Losing Uncle Tim, a book about the AIDS crisis, wins the first-ever Lambda Literary Award in the Children's/YA category

1970

The first Albert Whitman issues book, *How Do I Feel?* by Norma Simon, is published

1956

Three states boycott the company after it publishes *Fun for Chris*, a book about integration

1942

The Boxcar Children is published

1938

Pecos Bill: The Greatest Cowboy of All Time wins a Newbery Honor Award

1919

Albert Whitman & Company is started

Early 1900s

Albert Whitman begins his career in publishing

Celebrate with us in 2019!
Find out more at www.albertwhitman.com.